GALILEAN CHRISTIANITY

STUDIES IN BIBLICAL THEOLOGY

GALILEAN CHRISTIANITY

by

L. E. ELLIOTT-BINNS

SCM PRESS LTD
56 BLOOMSBURY STREET
LONDON

First published 1956

Printed in Great Britain by
Robert Cunningham and Sons Ltd.
Longbank Works, Alva

CONTENTS

PREFACE

In his inaugural lecture as Dean Ireland's Professor at Oxford in
1896 Dr Lock pointed out that not only did the Church pass
through a tunnel between the last quarter of the first century and
the middle of the second, but that a similar 'tunnel' existed between the death of our Lord and the beginning of the active work
of St Paul.[1] In what follows I have made suggestions which,
among other things, may do something to throw light on this
period, or, at least, to point to a new way of approach.

There has in recent years been a fresh interest both on the
Continent and in this country, in early Jewish Christianity; and
there are now signs of what seems to me a healthy tendency to
move away from the excessive scepticism, of which Bultmann is
a leading exponent, about the records of primitive Christianity
as a whole.

My own special interest in early Jewish Christianity goes back
to the years before the war when it was discussed in a seminar
held by Professor Burkitt, and for some time past I have been
working on a large-scale commentary on the Epistle of St James,[2]
approaching it especially from the Jewish angle; the present
volume, indeed, grew out of what was intended to be an essay
appended to that commentary.

The opinions here expressed were arrived at independently as
the result of much pondering over the problems raised by James,
and above all the kind of readers to whom it was addressed.
These, it seemed to me, were the men who had been the followers
of Jesus in Galilee during His lifetime. Standing apart from the
developments of Jewish Christianity in Jerusalem and from those
associated with the name of St Paul if they yet knew of them,
they remained faithful to the simple teaching they had received
from Jesus. Once having arrived at this theory I found support

---

[1] See *The Bible and Christian Life*, pp. 97f.
[2] Some of the statements in this essay, in a summary form, will receive fuller
exposition in the Commentary with a discussion of the evidence in detail.

for it in various quarters, and not least in some of the traditions lying behind the Synoptists. Further reading has shewn me that not dissimilar conclusions, such as those of Windisch and Lohmeyer, had been reached by others.

Two recent volumes, published since this essay was completed, seem to lend it incidental support. Martin Buber in *Two Types of Faith* sets out to shew that Israel and Primitive Christianity, as seen in a small group of Jewish Christians of whom the Synoptists are representative, held one type of 'faith', whilst Hellenistic Christianity, following St Paul, adopted another. Then K. Stendahl in *The School of St Matthew* suggests that the Gospel of Matthew was a kind of manual of instruction and administration emanating from that 'school', which itself went back to the school of Jesus. Some such school of Jesus might well represent Galilean Christianity.

Although lack of space prevents any discussion, mention should here be made of the interesting suggestion, which goes back at least as far as September 1923 when it was put forward by Edwyn Hoskyns in an article in *Theology*, and recently advocated with much learning and persuasiveness by G. H. Boobyer,[1] that Galilee in the Gospels is sometimes used symbolically of the Gentile world. I myself do not accept this view, however, and welcome the implications behind some recent remarks of the editors of *The Expository Times* (LXVI, p. 66):

> Is it possible that, after a generation deeply influenced by Form Criticism, and in spite of the present lure of Typology as expounded by Dr Austin Farrer, we are entering into a more constructive period? Have we parted with the delusion that the earliest tradition consisted of a formless mass of isolated stories, that the Marcan outline is no more than a literary construction, and that after Pentecost the original eyewitnesses of the Galilean Ministry were afflicted with a persistent form of dumbness?

[1] 'Galilee and the Galileans in St Mark's Gospel' (*Bulletin of the John Rylands Library*, XXXV, pp. 334ff). He concludes that Galilee was 'the land from which the disciples were to initiate that mission which would result chiefly in the conversion of the Gentiles.... The dominical mandate (14.28, 16.7) ... was in the nature of a charge ... to enter fully upon their divinely appointed missionary responsibilities' (p. 348). See further C. F. Evans in *J.T.S.*, N.S., V. pp. 3ff and Austin Farrer *A Study of St Mark*, Chapters vi and xiii.

The suggestions contained in this small volume are not put forth as irrefragable conclusions, but rather as tentative hypotheses for the consideration of other workers in the same field. I need hardly say that I should value extremely any comments and criticisms which they may be good enough to make upon them. Meanwhile I should like to express my gratitude to Professor W. Manson and Principal Matthew Black, both of whom read the manuscript and made fruitful suggestions, and also to the readers of the S.C.M. Press.

L. E. ELLIOTT-BINNS

Freshwell House
Saffron Walden
Essex

INTRODUCTION

ALTHOUGH Christianity had its origin in Galilee, the centre of
the movement soon shifted to Jerusalem, and the later books of
the N.T. practically ignore its presence and fortunes in Galilee.
This neglect continued in the early Church, and, indeed, until
quite recent times. Even among scholars little interest has been
taken in those who first heard the Gospel message and their subsequent fate. The only exception I can recall is Schmiedel's
casual remark that St Paul's teaching on redemption entirely
leaves out of account the men who sought and found forgiveness
and peace of soul in Jesus before His death.[1]

The Tübingen school of criticism tried to explain the history
of the primitive Church on the basis of a conflict between St
Paul, on the one hand, and the Twelve, especially St Peter, on
the other. But a more convincing case, I would suggest, can be
made out for a division between the early followers of Jesus in
Galilee, probably including some at least of the Twelve, and the
narrower Judaistic Christianity which was growing up at Jerusalem under the leadership of St James. That there was a distinction
between them was recognized by Streeter when he wrote:
'Judaistic Christianity should be regarded as the Christianity, not
so much of the Twelve, as of James' (*The Primitive Church*, p. 44).

Evidence for some kind of rivalry between Galilee and Jerusalem can clearly be seen in the N.T. itself, which contains what
appear to be irreconcilable traditions as to the scene of the post-
resurrection appearances of Jesus; and in the Gospel records there
is a noteworthy difference of emphasis, with, on the one side,
Mark, Q, some of the matter peculiar to Matthew,[2] and on the
other, matter peculiar to Luke (and the early chapters of Acts)
and John.

---

[1] Quoted Holzmann *Lehrbuch der N.T. Theologie*, II, p. 111.
[2] Other parts peculiar to Matthew seem to reflect 'not primitive Jewish Christianity, but a later Judaistic reaction against Petro-Pauline liberalism' (Streeter, *The
Four Gospels*, p. 512). Such passages, it may be suggested, come from the editor of
the Gospel, and not from what may be called the Matthean Logia.

I wish to suggest that in certain of the sources which underlie the Synoptic Gospels, and also in the Epistle of St James (which has striking resemblances with them both in outlook and teaching) we have evidence for a type of Christianity which continued to prevail in Galilee among the original followers of the Master; a type of Christianity which remained immune to developments which were taking place in the more prominent species of Jewish Christianity whose headquarters were at Jerusalem, immune also to the teaching of St Paul. Its influence on the form taken by Jewish Christianity was greater than is sometimes recognized, and for this reason, if for no other, its rise and subsequent development demand further study.

The original connexion of Christianity with Galilee, it need hardly be said, though it was largely ignored, was never entirely forgotten. How could it be among those who were readers of the Gospels? Moreover the term 'Galilean' seems in early days to have been used to describe the followers of Jesus; in Acts 1.11 the apostles are addressed as 'Ye men of Galilee' and it was only at a later stage and at Antioch that the term 'Christian' first came into use (Acts 11.26). Harnack restricted the term to the Gentile followers of Jesus; 'neither at first nor for a long while to come, were Jewish Christians designated by this name' (*Mission and Expansion* etc., I, p. 60). Rackham, commenting on Acts 11.26 (*Westminster Commentaries*, p. lxiii), thought that the earliest name for the disciples had been 'Nazareans' or 'Galileans'. Weizäcker, however, rejected the use of 'Galileans', holding that they were known as 'Nazarenes',[1] though not on account of the supposed origin of the founder (*Das apost. Zeitalter*, I, pp. 46f). The later Nazarenes, mentioned by Epiphanius, are said to have been descended from the followers of John the Baptist, and Professor Black has suggested that its use for Christians may 'have arisen through their popular identification with the followers and movement of John the Baptist' (*An Aramaic Approach to the Gospels and Acts*, p. 146).

Harnack accepted the title of 'Galileans' as descriptive of the first followers of Jesus, regarding it, however, as 'primarily a geo-

[1] On the different Greek forms of the word and their derivation, see Moulton, *Grammar of N.T. Greek*, II, pp. 107, 149f, Vincent Taylor, *St Mark*, pp. 177f and M. Black, *An Aromaic Approach*, etc., pp. 143f.

graphical term, but . . . also intended to throw scorn on the disciples as semi-pagans.'[1] Perhaps for this reason the term does not seem to have been much used in the early Church; Justin can even refer to a sect of Galileans to whom he denies the name of Christians (*Dial.* 80). They were possibly followers of Judas of Galilee (cf. Acts 5.37, Josephus *Ant.* XVIII.i.1, *Bell. Jud.* II. viii.1). To Hegesippus also (in Eusebius *Hist. Eccles.* IV.xxii.7) the Galileans were a Jewish, not a Christian, sect. The name, it would seem, was chiefly employed by non-Christians. In *Acta Theodati Ancyrani* XXXI we are told that the heathen called Jesus 'a ringleader of the Galileans', whilst Epictetus referred to His followers as 'Galileans' (Arrian *Diss.* IV.vii.6). Even if the dying cry of the Emperor Julian is apocryphal, his supposed use of the term 'Galilean' to describe the founder of Christianity (Gregory of Nazianzus *Orat.* IV) is evidence of its continued survival in pagan circles.

For the neglect of Christianity in Galilee a number of reasons may be adduced. In the early days of the Church there seems to have been a deliberate attempt to belittle Galilee in favour of Jerusalem, and in later times the fact that the Church was becoming more and more Gentile in its membership caused a lack of interest in the Jewish phase of Christianity, and Christianity in Galilee must have been almost purely Jewish.[2]

As the movement spread into a wider world there was perhaps also a desire to conceal its humble beginnings in a remote corner of the Empire. Traces of such an attitude can already be discerned in Acts, which tries to shew 'that Christianity, though no doubt it began in Palestine, is not really a Jewish but a universal religion' (Streeter, *The Four Gospels*, p. 538).[3] Acts, if it recognizes that the Gospel began in Galilee (10.37) and mentions a number of places in Palestine (Samaria, Joppa, Gaza, Caesarea, and even Tyre and Sidon), makes no reference to any Galilean locality. This omission, however, may have no significance, since such localities lay outside the scope of the narrative. The writings of St Paul, which

[1] *Op. cit.*, II, p. 5. For 'despised Galileans' cf. Acts 2.7; 3.6; 4.10; 24.5; John 1.46; 7.41f, 52.

[2] G. Schrenk, *Galiläa zur Zeit Jesu*, p. 17, however, thinks that those to whom Jesus spoke, even in the synagogues, may have included Gentiles.

[3] B. S. Easton, *Early Christianity*, pp. 43ff, on the other hand, tries to shew that one of the primary motives of Acts was to represent Christianity as a school of Judaism, and therefore a *religio licita*.

form so large a part of the surviving literature and perhaps for this reason may give rise to an unbalanced notion of conditions in the early Church, naturally share this universal outlook. There were other reasons also why St Paul should ignore Galilee, for his conception of Jesus led him to take no very great interest in the earthly life of the Master, nor, as a consequence, in the scene of His terrestrial activities. The fourth Gospel, whoever was its author, almost certainly came from the neighbourhood of Ephesus, and though it exhibits an intimate knowledge on some points of the ministry of Jesus, it entirely subordinates Galilee to Jerusalem. The evangelist 'is writing for a Church . . . which is too far from Palestine to be interested in Galilee' (W. L. Knox, *Some Hellenistic Elements in Primitive Christianity*, p. 61).

I

GALILEE IN THE TIME OF JESUS

To understand the origins of Christianity in Galilee, and the form which it there assumed, it is necessary to know something of contemporary conditions and especially of the outlook and composition of the population.

But first something must be said of its boundaries, which at all times appear to have been somewhat indefinite. In early days Galilee signified the small region round Kadesh; but by the time of Isaiah it also included the territories of Zebulon and Naphthali, and even parts of Asher and Issachar. In our Lord's day uncertainty still persisted, and Josephus himself is far from clear as to where its southern boundary occurred. In *Bell. Jud.* III.iii.1 he places it on the upper edge of the Plain of Esdraelon, but in Section 4 of the same passage he states that Samaria only extended to the lower edge of the plain.[1] In the Mishnah three distinct regions in Galilee are distinguished: Upper, Lower, and the Valley (that is the part round Tiberias). It is the latter region in which we are specially interested, and above all in the neighbourhood of the Lake; for the Galilean ministry of Jesus, save for occasional excursions east of the Lake and to the north, was confined to that area.[2]

(a) The Land

Josephus has preserved for us a vivid picture of Galilee as it was in his time, and it suggests much wealth and prosperity. He speaks of the rich and fertile soil, especially in the region round the Lake, a soil so productive that even the slothful were moved to cultivate it, of its many trees, of numerous and well-populated

[1] He also includes places east of the Lake, and even states that at one time Mount Carmel, which now belonged to Tyre, had been included.
[2] Lohmeyer, *Galiläa und Jerusalem*, p. 27, speaks of a 'christliche Galiläa' which included places such as Tyre and Sidon, Caesarea Philippi and the Decapolis; cf. p. 80 where Mount Hermon and possibly Damascus are included.

villages and many cities (*Bell. Jud.* III.iii.2, x.8, *Ant.* XVIII.ii.3).

This description, although true in essentials, must be taken as rather overdrawn and too favourable. None the less Galilee, if not outstandingly rich, was a prosperous land, and it had in addition sufficient trade to make it self-supporting and independent. No doubt it had suffered from deforestation and from the erosion of the soil which was constantly being washed down into the valleys, leaving the higher parts denuded; but it was still abundantly fertile, and it had a much better water supply than Judaea, and also received heavy dews from distant Hermon (cf. Ps. 133.3). Even to-day the soil is deep and rich and contains elements of the detritus of volcanic rock.[1]

Farming was carried on by many small-holders who owned their plots but probably found conditions hard, since the land and its products were subject to heavy taxation. There was in consequence a drift to the towns, a movement which had already been in progress for more than a century.[2] The methods of cultivation were traditional and wasteful, and the productivity of the soil was declining in consequence; and there was the ever present menace of bad harvests (an old state of affairs: cf. Isa. 3.14f; 5.8). They had also to suffer competition from large landowners using slave labour.[3]

In the Epistle of James, in spite of the interest taken in agriculture and in the rights of hired labourers, there is no mention of slave labour nor any suggestion that it existed. But it seems certain that it was there. G. F. Moore goes so far as to maintain that 'in the fertile and populous Galilee especially there were many heathen slaves and even considerable slave-households'; though he considers that hired servants were much more numerous in both households and husbandry.[4] Hired labourers, according to the O.T., were paid by the day (Lev. 19.13; Deut. 24.14f) and often, though not invariably (cf. Matt. 20.2) in kind. St Luke was evidently ignorant of this custom for in 10.7 he speaks of *wages* ($\mu\iota\sigma\theta\acute{o}\varsigma$) where Matt. 10.10 has *keep* ($\tau\rho o\phi\acute{\eta}$). In later times payment might be made by a draft on a shopkeeper or a money-

---

[1] See E. W. G. Masterman, *Studies in Galilee*, p. 17.
[2] *Letter of Aristeas*, § 108.
[3] Finkelstein says that the landowners were mainly Sadducees, *Harvard Theo. Rev.* XXII, p. 189.
[4] *Judaism*, II, pp. 137ff.

16

changer (*Baba Metzia* ix.12). At certain seasons of the year there would be urgent need to hire additional labour which would be supplied by peasant proprietors or by men from the towns (cf. Matt. 20.1ff).

The Lake had its fishing industry which brought much prosperity. Fish were pickled and salted at Tarichaea[1] before being exported, not only to Jerusalem, but to regions farther afield, and even to Rome itself.[2] The numerous roads[3] which traversed Galilee, including those from Damascus to Egypt and from Damascus to the coast, gave opportunities for traffic and commerce. Jewish trading with Gentiles was, however, restricted owing to religious scruples (*Aboda Zara* i.1ff); but the Galileans were probably not so meticulous in such matters as their brethren in Judaea although the Palestinian Talmud (*Kethuboth* 29b) says that they were not greatly concerned with worldly prosperity, and unlike the Judeans attached more importance to honour than to mammon. This may have been so in later times; but it is not the impression we gain from the Gospels (cf. Matt. 6.31f) or from the Epistle of James. The fact that Galilee was in close touch with Gentiles and that there were Greek cities in the neighbourhood must have meant that life for many was less strict, and that standards were not quite so high, save for the few who would react against pagan influences. The nearness of Judaea to the desert, which is nowhere seen from Galilee, might also add a touch of austerity to the men of the South.

(b) Galilee and its Inhabitants

Conditions in Galilee and the outlook and character of its inhabitants, as in other lands, were not merely affected by the present, but also by the past. We must therefore now turn to a brief survey of its previous history.

Upper Galilee had never been predominantly Jewish,[4] and a

---

[1] This is still an important industry; see Masterman, *op. cit.*, pp. 37ff.
[2] '*Aboda Zara* ii.6, *Nedarim* vi.4, Herodotus ix.120, Strabo XVI.ii.
[3] See further G. Adam Smith, *Hist. Geog. of the Holy Land*, pp. 425ff, and Masterman, *op. cit.*, pp. 10f.
[4] G. A. Barton: 'Danel, a Pre-Israelite Hero of Galilee' in *Memorial Lagrange* (1940) put forward the theory that the Danel of the Ras Shamra tablets was an eponym of the tribes of Dan and Zebulon. The theory is ingenious but not convincing and has been severely criticized; e.g. by R. de Langhe, *Les Textes de Ras Shamra-Urgarit* (1945), II, pp. 149ff.

large native population survived the occupation of Zebulon and
Naphthali (Judg. 1.30, 33). There was even a small and isolated
colony of Sidonians at Laish (Judg. 18.7, 28). From the first a
difference of race between the peoples of Northern and Southern
Israel seems to have existed. In Galilee the foreign elements were
mainly Canaanite, whilst in Judah they were largely Arab (e.g.
the Kenites), though Gen. 38.1f suggests some Canaanite mixture.[1] From its geographical position Judah was more subject to
Egyptian influences, whilst Israel naturally lay open to those
from Syria. There were even considerable differences of dialect
and if we had the Hebrew O.T. in its original form, before the
Massorites had done their work of unifying the grammar and
pointing, such differences would undoubtedly be more prominent; even as it is there are definite traces of a distinctive Northern
dialect.[2]

In the days of Isaiah Galilee was the 'circuit' (*galil*) of the
Gentiles (9.1), possibly because it was surrounded by Phœnicians,
Syrians, and other non-Hebrew peoples. Then came the Assyrian
conquest and the deportation of a large part of the population,
and their replacement by colonists from other lands (II Kings
15.29; 17.24ff). But many of the original inhabitants must have
remained, and these would retain memories of a time when Israel
was more powerful than Judah, remember too that Israel had
been the scene of the activities of great prophets like Elijah and
Elisha. So local patriotism and religious pride would be maintained.

After the fall of Jerusalem in 586 B.C. had reduced Judah to the
same level of misfortune as Israel there seems to have been a
drawing together of North and South (cf. Jer. 3.11; 23.6;
41.5) and Ezekiel could even contemplate their becoming a

[1] For the racial mixture in Judah see P. Haupt in *O.L.Z.*, xii, pp. 162f, and F.
Böhl, *Kanaanäer und Hebräer*, p. 98.
[2] Cf. Burney, *Kings*, pp. 208ff, Driver, *Int. to Lit. of O.T.*, p. 188. H. S. Nyberg,
(*Studien zum Hoseabuche*) believes that the text of Hosea is not so corrupt as is generally supposed, its obscurities being due to the use of North Israelite dialect. This
may also account for some of the peculiarities in Nahum. The Song of Songs is
possibly a Northern composition, and C. H. Gordon, *Ugaritic Literature*, p. 133,
thinks that Ecclesiastes was also a product of the North. Many of the so-called
Aramaisms in Hebrew may be survivals of the Northern dialect (see Meyer, *Die
Israeliten und ihre Nachbarstämme*, p. 491). Some of the peculiarities may be preserved
in the Samaritan version: cf. A. Sperber in *Heb. Union College Annual* (1937-8), pp.
151f, and C. Heller, *The Samaritan Pent.*, pp. 186ff.

united nation under a single ruler (37.15ff); but after the return
from the Exile the Northern people were despised and suspected as not being of sufficiently pure Hebrew stock. It has,
however, to be remembered that Judah itself became subject
to Edomite and Nabatean infiltration, even as far north as
Bethlehem.[1]

Coming down to Maccabean times we learn of fighting in
Galilee (I Mac. 5.14f, 17, 20, 23, 55; 12. 47); but those who
were recognized as genuine Jews were only a small proportion of
the inhabitants and were removed, with their possessions, to the
neighbourhood of Jerusalem; a long trek which must have involved much hardship for those who were compelled to undertake
it. Galilee was left as a heathen land. Under John Hyrcanus (135-
105) the Jewish state began once more to expand and Galilee
was reconquered. Then, or soon afterwards, Galilee was closely
incorporated and its inhabitants given the choice of expulsion or
circumcision. Most of them seem to have accepted the latter
alternative, and gradually merged with the Jewish people; but
originally the Galileans, the folk from whom the first Christians
were drawn, were largely of non-Jewish descent. The process of
Judaizing and training the new converts was no doubt carried
out by the establishment of schools and synagogues, probably
under Pharisaic control, and seems to have been highly successful.[2]
Surrounded as they were by people of other races and hostile
religions the men of Galilee naturally developed a tenacious love
of their own nationality and customs, and a stern resolve to preserve and maintain their independence. This sturdy patriotism
would be all the more necessary in view of the large pagan population. What proportion the Jewish and Gentile parts bore to one
another it is impossible to say; Moulton thought that the Gentiles
were actually in a majority,[3] and though this seems an exaggera-
tion there can be no doubt that they provided a large element.[4]

[1] See Meyer, *Entstehung des Judentums*, pp. 165ff.

[2] In 57 B.C. Gabinius, to weaken Jerusalem, divided the country into five districts,
each with a capital and Sanhedrin of its own, of which one was Sepphoris. The
scheme was soon abandoned, but the local councils seem to have retained some
influence. See A. Schlatter, *Gesch. Israels* (ed. 3), pp. 428f.

[3] *Grammar of N.T. Greek*, II, pp. 12f. It may be recalled that Houston Stewart
Chamberlain, *The Foundations of the Nineteenth Century*, I, p. 210 maintained that as
Jesus was a Galilean He must have been of Aryan stock.

[4] Strabo, writing early in the first century A.D., describes Galilee as containing
Egyptians, Arabians and Phœnicians (XVI.ii.34).

The command in Matt. 10.5, 'Go not into *any* way of the Gentiles', even if it applied to Palestine as a whole, seems evidence in support of this.

The danger from pagan influences must have been enhanced when the Herods, with their strong Hellenistic sympathies, became rulers of the land, whilst the close proximity of the Decapolis with its Greek inhabitants[1]—the swine of Gadara[2] (Mark 5.1ff), suggest a non-Jewish population—helped in the same direction. A further reinforcement must have come from the cities which the Herods established in Galilee, although these may not have greatly affected the common people of the countryside. The Herods had their first capital in Galilee at Sepphoris, making it αὐτοκρατορίδα (Josephus *Ant.* XVIII.ii.1); later they moved it to Tiberias,[3] the site of the ancient Raqqath.[4] At first Tiberias was a purely Gentile city,[5] for Jews were reluctant to settle in a place part of whose foundations covered a burial ground. Josephus describes the inhabitants as a promiscuous collection (σύγκλυδες), but says that they included many Galileans. Herod compelled unwilling settlers to take up residence there, and these included some people of standing (τῶν ἐν τέλει). Tiberias was famous for its medicinal springs and baths; the elder Pliny speaks of *Tiberiada aquis calidis salubre* (*Hist. Nat.* v.15). These baths still existed when Sir John Maundeville visited Palestine in 1322, and even to-day the springs are noted for their medicinal properties. The ruins of Tiberias, which extend far beyond the boundaries of the modern city, shew that it once covered a considerable area. Not far away was another city of some size, Tarichaea, which like Tiberias stood between the hills and the Lake (*Bell. Jud.* III.x.1). Most scholars, following Pliny's description, have placed it in the south-eastern corner of the Lake, but Dalman favours Magdala.[6] An even earlier city was Bethsaida,

---

[1] Any mention of the Decapolis is avoided in rabbinic writings. Little is known of its organization or the part which it played in Palestinian life: see Guthe, *Die griech. römischen Städte des Ostjordanlandes.*

[2] Gadara was an important centre of learning and letters.

[3] Schürer said not earlier than A.D. 26, but the evidence of coins places it at least as early as 22: see G. A. Smith, *Hist. Geog.*, p. 448, note 2.

[4] Neubauer, *Géog. du Talmud*, p. 208.

[5] This no doubt was the reason for no mention of Tiberias in the Synoptic Gospels.

[6] *Sacred Sites and Ways*, p. 126, note 8.

just across the Jordan,[1] which Herod Philip founded in 3 B.C., transforming it from a mere village (*Ant.* XVIII.ii.1).

(c) Languages

A very interesting and most important question regarding Galilee concerns the languages in use there. Professor Black considers that whilst Aramaic was the common speech, Greek would also be needed for cultural and commercial purposes, whilst Latin would be the language of the army, and to a less degree of commerce. He thinks that Hebrew was also cultivated 'as a spoken tongue in the learned coteries of the Rabbis'.[2] There is little doubt that Aramaic[3] was the popular speech, though the pronunciation of the Galileans aroused the scorn and contempt of the Jews, especially the slurring of gutturals.[4] The rabbis considered that this defective pronunciation precluded Galileans from studying the Law (T. B. *Erubin* 63b) and Galileans were sometimes forbidden to recite the public prayers in the synagogue (T. B. *Megillah* 24b).

Whilst most scholars are agreed that Aramaic was the common speech, considerable difference of opinion exists as to how far Greek was in use. It would certainly be much more needed in Galilee than in Judaea.[5] G. F. Moore, however, deprecates the idea that many Galileans were bilingual, considering that in any case religious topics would be discussed only in Aramaic.[6] It is certainly interesting to note that Josephus originally wrote his *Wars of the Jews* in Aramaic, and then translated it into Greek for the benefit of those under Roman rule (*Bell. Jud.* Proem. i.1).[7] In this work he had the assistance of others, as his own knowledge of Greek was inadequate to the task (*Contra Apionem* i.9).

Even if intercourse with Greek towns and their Gentile inhabitants was avoided for patriotic reasons, a knowledge of Greek,

[1] The idea that there was also a 'western' Bethsaida is now generally abandoned; see Dalman, *op. cit.*, p. 176.

[2] *An Aramaic Approach to the Gospels and Acts*, p. 13.

[3] On Aramaic dialects see Black, *op. cit.*, pp. 17ff, Neubauer, *Géog. du Talmud*, pp. 184ff, and *Studia Biblica*, I, pp. 49ff.

[4] For examples of absurd blunders arising from Galilean peculiarities see Edersheim, *Life and Times of Jesus the Messiah*, I, p. 225.

[5] Cf. Moulton in *Cambridge Biblical Essays*, p. 488.

[6] *Judaism*, III, pp. 53f.

[7] Many scholars think that the work in its present Greek form is more than a bare translation and that considerable matter was added to it.

even if only superficial, would be so useful that the opportunity of acquiring it must have been seized by many. Dalman goes so far as to affirm that 'anyone brought up in Bethsaida would not only have understood Greek, but would have been polished through intercourse with foreigners, and have some Greek culture'[1]; he suggests further that the careless pronunciation of Aramaic by the Galileans may have been due to the widespread use of Greek.[2] So, too, Moulton has the rather odd idea that the Greek of St Peter might well have been better than his Aramaic.[3] Hort once made the interesting suggestion that there was a special type of Palestinian Greek, at least so far as vocabulary was concerned, attributing to it such words as προσωπολημψίαις (Jas. 2.1, etc.) and ψυχική (3.15, etc.).

Thus the experts are divided, and those of us who are not experts cannot be expected to decide between them. It seems probable, however, that on the whole many of the inhabitants of Galilee had some knowledge of both Greek and Aramaic.

[1] *Op. cit.*, p. 165.   [2] *Jesus-Jeshua*, pp. 2ff.
[3] *Grammar of N.T. Greek*, II, p. 26.

II

THE GALILEAN MINISTRY

THAT a Jewish teacher should have chosen Galilee as the scene of his main activities seems at first sight rather anomalous. Jerusalem, the religious capital of the people, was the obvious centre for proclaiming any new development of Judaism intended to make a popular appeal, and also the appropriate stage for Messianic action.[1] It is, of course, conceivable that Jesus definitely considered beginning His ministry in the Holy City (cf. Matt. 4.5; Luke 4.9) and then abandoned the idea, deciding in the end that Jerusalem was to be reserved for the scene of His final rejection and death. In any case the baptism and temptation took place before the ministry in Galilee.

There are, however, many reasons why Galilee should have been his choice. In the first place it was the district where He had been brought up,[2] and it was only natural that He should be anxious to deliver His message to those whom He knew; though He soon came to realize that a prophet had no honour in his own country (Mark 6.4; Matt. 13.57; John 4.44; the inclusion in the fourth Gospel is significant). Galilee, moreover, provided a wide field for evangelization. At the beginning of the Christian era it was a very different land from that we know to-day, even when recent Jewish activities are taken into account. It had a large and vigorous population, especially around the shores of the Lake, with many towns and villages.[3] In the Gospels, as G. A. Smith

---

[1] Cf. Loisy, Le quatrième Évangile, p. 64.
[2] See W. Bauer, 'Jesus der Galiläer' in Festgabe Jülicher, pp. 16ff. In the fourth Gospel, however, 'the Lord's fellow-countrymen, his own people, are the Jews rather than the Galileans, and his patris Judaea and Jerusalem, not Galilee or Nazareth' (R. H. Lightfoot, Locality and Doctrine etc., p. 146). The narrative in Matt. 2 apparently assumes that Bethlehem was the home of Joseph and Mary (contrast Luke 2.4) and that it was only after the return from Egypt that there was any thought of settling in Galilee (vv. 22f). In this case Jesus would not have been a Galilean by origin; as a descendant of David. He was a Judean.
[3] Josephus estimated the population in his day at three million (Vita 45, Bell. Jud., III.iii.12), a quite impossible figure, though Merrill, Galilee in the Time of Christ,

23

has observed, 'the noise of a close and busy life is always audible' (*Hist. Geog.*, p. 421).

The situation of Galilee was also favourable, for like Israel of old it was both central and retired. The merchant caravans kept it in touch with the outer world and the route from Damascus to the Mediterranean which ended at Acre passed close to the Lake; it may even have gone through Capernaum. At the same time there were tracts of country where quiet could be found which Jesus would use not only to find rest for His tired spirit, but also as a background for the training of the apostles, a task which seems to have been the principal object of His later ministry,[1] though this can hardly have influenced His earlier choice of Galilee. Judaea and the neighbourhood of Jerusalem would have provided no comparable opportunities, and had He remained there His followers might well have been confused with those of John the Baptist[2]; Jerusalem, moreover, was full of religious teachers, each with his own following.

Galilee also had advantages in the matter of climate, at least in the tropical basin in which the Sea of Galilee is situated. There were, it need scarcely be pointed out, immense differences of temperature in Galilee which also included the lofty heights of Naphthali,[3] but for our purposes the district round the Lake need alone be considered where, even in winter, the temperature normally remains high. This mild climate and the long spells of fine weather made it an ideal land for carrying on an open-air mission, giving as it did opportunities for people to travel long distances to hear the new teacher, even when this might involve spending a night on the way. In addition the cultivation of the vine and olive, important activities in Galilee, do not require attention at all seasons, and so many would be free to leave their usual occupations for a time.

The main reason, however, which led Jesus to choose Galilee

p. 62, was disposed to accept it. The land, however, could never have supported such numbers and there are no traces of extensive ruins. Masterman, *Studies in Galilee*, concluded that 400,000 would be a generous estimate. Even this was a sufficiently large population amidst which to proclaim the new message.

[1] See Bruce, *The Training of the Twelve*, and Latham, *Pastor Pastorum*.

[2] Cf. above, p. 12.

[3] See G. A. Smith, *op. cit.*, p. 72, and the list of temperatures, p. 677. The notices of the warmth of the fire during our Lord's trial in Mark 14.54 and John 18.25 may reflect a Galilean outlook. But winters could be severe even in Galilee and Masterman speaks of them as 'cold, wet, lifeless', *op. cit.*, p. 137.

was almost certainly the greater freedom which it provided, both on account of the distance from Jerusalem and also because of the character of its inhabitants. We have already noticed the difference between Galileans and Jews as a result of their derivation from diverse racial stocks and the effects of their different environments. This matter must now be treated at greater length, for it is essential that the differences between Jews and Galileans should be fully realized. In N.T. itself there is a recognition of the fact, for the term 'Jews' often serves to point the contrast. In Mark 7.3 it signifies those who came from Jerusalem, as it seems also to do in Matt. 28.15; Luke 7.3; 23.3ff. In the fourth Gospel there is a continual contrast between 'the Jews' and 'the crowd', the latter reflecting the spirit of Galilee as against 'the narrow finality of Judaism'.[1]

The most striking characteristic of the Galileans was their spirit of independence, especially when compared with the Judeans. This was due in part to their economic position, for agriculture and the thriving trade in fish made them more self-supporting than their southern neighbours. Life in that fertile land was simpler and more natural than in a great ecclesiastical city with its hampering customs and traditions. Everything seemed to combine to foster the distinction between them and the fact that the inhabitants of Jerusalem looked down on the Galileans —for them 'fool' and 'Galilean' were almost synonyms—served to perpetuate and intensify the division between them.[2]

Then again the traditions and usages of Galilee often varied from those in the south. They had different weights and measures, the Galilean *sela* weighed only half that of Judaea (*Keth.* v.9, *Hullin.* xi.2); and the prices of goods also differed.[3] There were also many variations in social and legal customs as in the case of removals (*Shebiith* ix.2), marriage (*Keth.* xii.10), vows (*Nedarim* ii.4) and usucaption (*Baba Bathra* iii.2). Even in religious observances the two were not fully at one, for the Galileans did no work on the eve of the Passover (*Pesahim* iv.5) and held a feast before the Day of Atonement (*Hullin* v.3).

The independent spirit of the Galileans made them hot tem-

---

[1] Westcott, *St John*, p. ix.
[2] The Jews hated the Samaritans; the Galileans they merely despised.
[3] Dalman, *Sacred Sites* etc., p. 7.

pered and ready to take offence (cf. Luke 9.54), they were all of them 'sons of thunder'; but at the same time they were more open to outside influences and prepared to make experiments. In far-off days when the two kingdoms of Judah and Israel existed side by side, the former remained ever faithful to the house of David, but in the latter there were continual changes of dynasty. This readiness to change seems to have descended to those who were the successors of Israel on the same soil, even if not exactly of identical lineage. Josephus described them as 'ever fond of innovations, and naturally disposed to changes, and as delighting in seditions' (*Vita* xvii., *Ant.* XVII.x.5, XX.vi.1, *Bell. Jud.* I.xvi.5, II.xvii.8), a judgement which was confirmed by Tacitus (*Ann.* xii.54).

We saw above that the Galileans because they lived at close quarters with Gentiles clung to their faith with fanatical determination. But they clung to it as a mark of separation; in other words they were nationalistically and not ecclesiastically minded, and though holding fast to their religion were by no means ready to submit to the rigid interpretations current in official quarters.[1] G. A. Smith suggested that one of the reasons why Jesus chose Galilee as the scene of His mission was the greater preparedness of the Galileans to receive the message that the Kingdom of heaven was at hand. Thus He could appeal to the spirit of patriotism, and at the same time endeavour to touch it to diviner issues.

The Galileans, partly owing to their distance from Jerusalem, but still more to their independence of spirit, were in general lax in their attitude towards strict orthodoxy and its demands. Such matters seemed too petty, and moreover they had their own traditions.[2] At a later date Galilean synagogues were notorious for unusual features, such as a northern orientation with the entrance to the south.[3] Synagogues belonging to our period have

---

[1] Josephus said of the followers of Judas of Galilee that although they accepted the teaching of the Pharisees they preserved their own freedom and recognized none but God as their ruler and lord (*Ant.* XVIII.i.6). Edersheim, *The Life and Times of Jesus the Messiah*, I, p. 238, said of the Galileans: 'Their enthusiasm could not be kindled by the logical subtleties of the Schools, but their hearts burned within them for their God, their land, their religion and their freedom.'

[2] The average Jew in Galilee probably paid scant respect to the numerous rules of Levitical purity: see Büchler in *The Expository Times*, XXI, pp. 34ff, and Abrahams in *Cambridge Biblical Essays*, p. 167.

[3] See S. A. Cook, *Schweich Lectures*, pp. 209ff, and Masterman, *op. cit.*, pp. 209ff.

entirely disappeared, but those which have survived may well preserve earlier characteristics.

Thus Galilee would provide a freer atmosphere and its distance from the capital would mean that Jesus was outside the direct cognizance of the religious authorities in Jerusalem. They did, indeed, send down emissaries to report upon Him (Mark 7.1f; cf. John 1.19), but they seem to have had little effect upon local opinion. Jesus and His disciples might be criticized for failing to observe the customary rules as to washing the hands before meals (Mark 7.1ff; Matt. 15.1ff, 20), but apparently this did not prevent men from sitting down at table with them.[1]

One further factor should I think be considered—the living interest which in our Lord's day and immediately before it was exhibited by the Galileans in religious development. The evidence for this is to be found in the considerable number of apocryphal works coming from writers in that region. It is evident that in the centuries before the Christian era Galilee was the scene of a quite considerable spiritual movement by which the ideas of the O.T. received a new and fruitful interpretation; an interpretation, moreover, in a direction which may be called Christian. When Jesus began His mission in Galilee He would find many minds in which His message, even though in only a rudimentary form, was already at work. 'It is significant that it was not from Judaea, the stronghold of Pharisaic legalism, but from Galilee, the land of the religious mystic and seer, that Christ and eleven of His apostles derived their origin and their religious culture.'[2] This circumstance has also immense importance for the subsequent history of Christianity in Galilee; men who were conscious of rich and deep-seated traditions of their own would not readily submit, even when Christians, to the dictates of Jerusalem; especially if the Christians at Jerusalem found it difficult, in their turn, to overcome an inborn prejudice against and contempt for Galileans. A division within Jewish Christianity thus seemed inevitable, for it corresponded to a very ancient cleavage.

[1] It is quite possible that the disciples omitted to wash their hands, not because they were followers of Jesus (and He justified their neglect), but simply as Galileans. W. Bauer in *Festgabe Jülicher*, p. 27, suggests that when St Peter ate with Gentiles at Antioch (Gal. 2.12) he was only doing what he had done all his life.

[2] Charles, *Between the Old and New Testaments*, p. 157.

According to the synoptic outline based on Mark[1] Jesus carried on His ministry almost entirely in Galilee until His last journey to Jerusalem, though in Luke there is a less decided emphasis on Galilee. In the fourth Gospel, however, a ministry in Jerusalem is much more prominent. The two traditions are not necessarily contradictory; the author of the fourth Gospel may have taken the Galilean ministry for granted, whilst the arrangement in Mark may not be strictly chronological or intended to be exhaustive.[2]

According to the Marcan outline Jesus is represented as taking up the message of John the Baptist that the kingdom of heaven was at hand and giving to it a spiritual content, such as was rare in nationalist circles. Leaving Nazareth, which was perhaps too isolated to form a base,[3] He moved to Capernaum (rather suddenly mentioned in Mark 1.21) in the district at the north-west corner of the Lake. A period of great, if superficial, enthusiasm ensues aroused by the novelty of the teaching and the performance of mighty works; but this is followed by growing opposition on the part of the religious leaders, and finally by the withdrawal of Jesus from the multitude. Vincent Taylor considers that He had come to regard His ministry in Galilee as a failure (*St Mark*, p. 638), but not owing to waning popularity so much as to the facile nature of this popularity (*The Life and Ministry of Jesus*, pp. 129ff). This aspect of the ministry, which may have called forth 'real and passionate disappointment' (C. J. Cadoux, *The Hist. Mission of Jesus*, p. 192), seems to be emphasized in the fourth Gospel (e.g. John 6.66ff; 12.37ff), though similar admissions are found in Mark 6.5; Matt. 11.20ff; 12.45; 15.12. Other reasons may have contributed to the withdrawal which apparently took place after the murder of John the Baptist when Jesus crossed over to the eastern side of the Lake beyond Herod's jurisdiction, and then travelled to the north (Mark 6.29, 31; 7.24; Matt. 14.12f). Jesus

[1] Carrington in *The Church Quarterly Rev.* (1953), p. 218, suggests that Mark had before him a 'Judean' Gospel into which he fitted 'Petrine' and 'Galilean' material.

[2] Vincent Taylor, *The Life and Ministry of Jesus*, p. 39, thinks that though there are gaps in the Marcan outline it gives 'a convincing summary of the outstanding events in the life of Jesus'.

[3] Nazareth was not completely isolated, being connected by road with Capernaum and having near it the important *Via Maris*. It was, however, evidently a small and insignificant place which receives no mention in the O.T., Josephus, the Talmud and Midrash, though there are traces of it in later writings: see G. F. Moore, *Judaism*, III, p. 93.

probably wished to avoid political complications and the too ready activities of those who misunderstood His aims (cf. John 6.15). There does, however, seem to have been a change of method, for thenceforward He appears to have concentrated on the intensive training of the apostles.

Although Luke follows Mark in general outline he has a different point of view with a special interest in Samaria.[1] In Mark, and less clearly in Matthew, the last days in Jerusalem form 'a dark passage which must be traversed before the end is reached', but for Luke 'Jerusalem is the goal and the culminating scene of the Lord's activity'.[2]

Luke appears to have no sustained interest in Galilee,[3] such as is found in the other Synoptists; possibly because he was not a native, or because those for whom he wrote were ignorant of the country. He is not at pains to distinguish it from Judaea, and may even include it in the wider term which for him seemed equivalent to Palestine (Luke 1.5; 7.17; cf. 23.5; Acts 2.9; 10.37; 11.1,29; 26.20). In 4.44, quite against the context, he substitutes 'Judaea' for the 'Galilee' of Mark 1.39,[4] and in 4.23 he is content to summarize events at Capernaum which Mark records more fully. On the other hand it is St Luke who draws attention to the presence of women 'from Galilee' at the crucifixion and as performing the last sad offices (Luke 23.49, 55).

St Luke appears to have had no first-hand knowledge of Galilee, though in company with St Paul he must have spent some time in its neighbourhood. The fact that he goes out of his way to say that Capernaum is a city of Galilee, and Arimathaea a city of the Jews (Luke 4.31; 23.51), may be explained by the ignorance of his readers rather than by his own; but his use of τὴν ὀρεινήν in 1.39,[5] and the insertion of Bethsaida in

[1] R. H. Lightfoot, *Locality and Doctrine*, p. 133, pointed out that in Luke 275 verses are concerned with Galilee, 350 with Samaria, and 320 with Jerusalem. It is true that the 'great interpolation' begins in Samaria (9.51f) but much of it, if Matthean parallels can be trusted, actually occurred in Galilee. Creed, *St Luke*, p. 139, thought that 'very much of the contents . . . is not in place in a genuine journey . . . details suggest the background of the Galilean ministry'.

[2] Lightfoot, *op. cit.*, p. 143.

[3] For Luke's suppression of Galilean material see Foakes Jackson and Kirsopp Lake, *The Beginnings of Christianity*, I, pp. 302ff.

[4] The Received text agrees with Mark and its reading is retained even in the R.V. The best MSS. however are against it.

[5] Cf. Dalman, *Sacred Sites* etc., p. 52: 'No Galilean would have spoken in such a general way of a "hill-country".'

9.19,[1] reveal ignorance of the country. Significant also is his substitution of the 'Lake of Gennesaret' for the Sea of Galilee. On the other hand he is the only evangelist who records Pilate's slaughter of the Galileans (13.1), possibly because he required it to explain the rift between Pilate and Herod (23.6f, 12).

It may be, however, that the greater prominence given to Jerusalem in the third Gospel is due ultimately to the desire to give an artistic form to the work; the whole narrative being designed to move forward towards Jerusalem as its goal, just as in Acts it culminates in Rome.[2]

Whilst the Synoptic outline seems to confine the main preaching of Jesus to Galilee,[3] signs are not wanting in these Gospels that Jerusalem actually received greater attention than would appear on the face of the narrative. In Matt. 23.37; Luke 13.34, ποσάκις surely implies that the people of Jerusalem had had many opportunities of accepting Jesus; these can hardly have been covered by the 'daily teaching in the temple' of Mark 14.49. That there was an early ministry in Judaea which was brought to an end by the apprehension of John the Baptist is suggested by Mark 1.14, and even more by Matt. 4.12. Such a ministry may also have been abandoned in face of Pharisaic opposition (John 4.1). The fact that Jesus was on intimate terms with the family at Bethany (Mark 14.49) suggests that He had been frequently in the neighbourhood; though it is possible that He had known them before actually the ministry began, they may have been family friends visited during attendance at the feasts.

Though the ministry in Jerusalem is only noticed in connexion with the last days of the life of Jesus an immense mass of material is recorded concerning the period; Wellhausen (*Das Evangelium Marci*, p. 94) would extend the time spent there in order to find room for it. May it not be possible that material belonging to earlier visits has here been grouped together? The apparent neglect of Jerusalem by Jesus seems unlikely, and H. Scott

---

[1] The neighbourhood of so large a town would have rendered a miraculous supply of food quite unnecessary.

[2] B. S. Easton, *Early Christianity*, p. 55, thought that Luke [in Acts] deemed the supremacy of Jerusalem 'a paramount fact in Christianity'.

[3] It is remarkable that although Mark uses κηρύσσειν of the world-wide preaching of the Gospel in 13.10; 14.9 elsewhere he confines it (save of the Decapolis in 5.20) to Galilee (e.g. 1.14, 38f, 45; 3.14; 6.20; 7.36); see Lohmeyer, *Urchristentum*, I, pp. 53ff.

Holland (*The Philosophy of Faith*, pp. 128ff, 153f) argued strongly that a ministry in Jerusalem is implied in the Synoptic record and necessary to supplement it.

In the fourth Gospel there is an entirely different emphasis; it is the ministry in Jerusalem that receives prominence, and it is even stated that it was there that the Galileans themselves were first impressed by the work of Jesus (John 4.45), a statement which seems very significant, and in John 7.3 it is suggested that the bulk of His followers, if not the whole number, were in Judaea. After Chapter 7 there are but two casual references to Galilee (10.40f and 11.54).

But here again there are implications of unmentioned activity, such as the notices of several visits to Galilee (John 2.12ff; 4.1ff; 6.1ff; 7.1) for which, incidentally, no reason is given, and it was there that the two unique signs in the Gospel were performed and the shewing forth of the glory of Jesus began (John 2.1ff; 4.46ff). That the Synoptic Gospels were already in circulation when John wrote may be taken as certain, though whether he was acquainted with them is a point upon which critics have reached no agreement. It is, however, possible, not to say probable, that he knew them and wrote by way of supplement using material which they had passed over. Hoskyns considered that there was no desire on the part of the author to suppress the Galilean ministry, he simply took it for granted (*The Fourth Gospel*, p. 69). Hoskyns also accounts for the omission of any mention of Nazareth in 1.29 (cf. Mark 1.9, etc.) as due to a desire to emphasize 'the heavenly rather than the Galilean origin of Jesus' (*op. cit.*, p. 175). Moffatt thought that the author 'with his predilection for displaying the religion of Jesus in contrast to Jewish theories and objections naturally chose Jerusalem as the locus for his debates; the simpler Galilean preaching did not interest him.' (*Int. to the Literature of the N.T.*, ed. 3, p. 543.)

The author of the fourth Gospel certainly had no animus against the Galileans; on the contrary he contrasts the reception of Jesus in Galilee with His rejection in Jerusalem (4.43-5, if we take 'his own country' as meaning Jerusalem), and it was in Galilee that, as we have already noticed, the unique signs were performed.

I think we may conclude that though there is much that is obscure concerning the scenes of the ministry of Jesus most of the apparent contradictions can be resolved, but that in any case the traditional view which connects it so closely with Galilee still stands; it was the fulfilment of the prophecy of Isa. 9.1f (cf. Matt. 4.15f; Luke 1.79). Dodd considers that the 'emphasis on the beginning in Galilee seems to have been integral to the pattern of the *kerygma* from the first', and finds some significance in its strong persistence 'in face of the tendency to canonize Jerusalem as the place of the origin of the Christian mission'; see Luke 24.47, Acts 1.8, and perhaps even Rom. 15.19.[1]

[1] *According to the Scriptures*, pp. 80f, with the note.

III

THE NEW CENTRE AT JERUSALEM

WHEN Jesus entered Jerusalem on Palm Sunday He was accompanied according to the Synoptists, by great crowds of Galileans going up to the Passover. To regard these crowds as His adherents or even those who had been attracted by His teaching would be a grave mistake. Such no doubt were among them, but many more, having nationalist notions of the function of the Messiah, may have joined the multitude in the vague hope that He was about to proclaim Himself their leader.[1] Judas Iscariot, one must suppose, was not the only one to be disillusioned in this matter. In the fourth Gospel, however, the crowds are said to come from Jerusalem where enthusiasm may well have been stirred by the events which had recently taken place there, and above all by the story of the raising of Lazarus (12.9ff). But the crowds who came down from the city did not consist entirely or even mainly of its inhabitants, in fact they were made up of pilgrims to the feast who had arrived in advance (12.12). What more natural than for Galileans already in Jerusalem to flock out to welcome their own prophet? Thus there is no serious discrepancy between the different accounts.

Though many Galilean disciples may have gone up with Jesus and the apostles to His last Passover, many no doubt remained at home. Those who attended the feast, apart from the closer ring, would return when it was over. This would account for the few, one hundred and twenty only, who are mentioned at Pentecost (Acts 1.15); to take them as the whole of the Christian Church at the time, the sole results of the life-work of Jesus, is to hold a very meagre idea of its outcome. Were there not also

---

[1] There has perhaps been a tendency to over-emphasize the messianic aspect of the entry. In Matt. 21.11 Jesus is hailed, not as the Messiah, but as the prophet of Nazareth of Galilee. Mark 11.9f, seems more messianic, but it is not certain that ὁ ἐρχόμενος was then a messianic title: see Taylor *ad loc.*

five hundred brethren to whom He had appeared (I Cor. 15.6)? These may well have been Galileans.[1]

But if the great bulk of the followers of Jesus were normally resident in Galilee the headquarters of the movement were soon firmly fixed at Jerusalem. Of those who had accompanied Jesus the most prominent, including the eleven surviving apostles, remained there, or it may be returned after a short interval. The period between the resurrection and the ascension, as recorded by St Luke (Acts 1.4) was spent in Jerusalem and according to the same authority (Luke 24.50; Acts 1.12) the disciples had the last glimpse of their Master on the Mount of Olives.[2] The events of those days would give to Jerusalem a new significance and the time previously spent with Jesus in Galilee would be apt to seem of small importance by comparison. The ascension had taught the disciples to lift their thoughts above mere earthly things, and they had an intense realization of the continued, if unseen, presence of Jesus with them; and of the guidance of the Holy Spirit whom He had sent. Moreover He would soon return.

There was thus, almost at once, a shifting of interest as the old Galilean events retired into the background, and what had taken place at Jerusalem becomes all important. Harnack, who held that the Galilean accounts were earlier and alone authentic, considered that one result of the transition was the invention of legends emphasizing the importance of Jerusalem. 'Is it possible to conceive a stronger instance of the working over a narrative than that which we have in the Judean story of the childhood, and in the transference of the first appearance of the Risen Lord from Galilee to Jerusalem?' (*The Constitution and Law of the Church*, p. 29).

That Jerusalem, once it had become the centre of the new movement, should seek to discredit any rivals, or at least to assert her own predominance, was only natural. Such an attitude was deeply ingrained in the Holy City of the Jewish people. She had an inveterate jealousy of other religious centres and the old story

---

[1] 'The largeness of the numbers shews that this appearance was in Galilee and the reference in Matt. 28.16 to "the mountain where Jesus had appointed them" suggests that our Lord had appointed a rendezvous for His Galilean followers after His Resurrection.' Goudge in *Westminster Commentaries*.

[2] Matthew places the last charge to the disciples in Galilee and does not mention the ascension; instead there is the promise of the perpetual presence (Matt. 28.12ff).

of her relations with Shechem and with the Samaritans may well
have been repeated on a Christian stage. The new centre would
thus be strongly upheld by those resident there, and no doubt
the few Christian Jews of the Dispersion would accept the state
of affairs and regard the leaders at Jerusalem as the natural successors of the Sanhedrin and continue to forward their gifts to
them.[1] But there is evidence that the Galileans thought differently.
We have already noticed the different conception of the scene of
the ministry in the Synoptists and in St John, and the distinction
goes even deeper. For St Mark 'Galilee is the holy land of the
Gospel, the place of its eschatological fulfilment . . . Jerusalem is
the city of deadly enmity to Jesus, of sin, and of death.'[2] The
only miracle he records there is the cursing of the barren fig-tree
(Mark 11.12ff).[3]

J. Weiss (*Die Schriften des N.T.*, I., p. 208) finds an even
stronger assertion of the rights of Galilee in Mark 14.28, taking
'go before you into Galilee' to mean that Jesus would place Himself at the head of His followers and return thither to carry on
His new community. Vincent Taylor finds this suggestion very
attractive; but thinks that it is ruled out by the parallel in Mark
16.7 where προάγει cannot mean 'He is leading', but only 'He is
going before'. He concludes that the saying is an anticipation of
the resurrection appearances.[4]

Matthew has much the same view of the relations of Galilee
and Jerusalem, though with some modifications. For him 'the
divine counsel and election with regard to Galilee is solely
eschatological, whereas with regard to Jerusalem it is continuous
and historically age-long'[5]; for him Galilee is the birth-place of
the Christian Church, and, as for Mark, the Holy Land where
Jesus had revealed Himself.[6]

---

[1] Cf. Schweitzer, *The Mysticism of St Paul*, p. 156.

[2] Lohmeyer, *Galiläa und Jerusalem*, pp. 29 and 34. Cf. the similar statement by
R. H. Lightfoot, *Locality and Doctrine* etc., pp. 124f.

[3] Ed. Meyer, *Ursprung und Anfänge des Christentums*, II, p. 442 note 5.

[4] *St Mark*, p. 549. Lightfoot also rejects the idea (*op. cit.*, p. 52). Lohmeyer thought
that they were to go to Galilee to witness the parousia, not merely the post-resurrection appearances (*op. cit.*, pp. 10ff, *Evangelium des Markus*, pp. 312, 356; cf. Lightfoot,
op. cit., pp. 61ff and 73ff).

[5] Lightfoot, *op. cit.*, p. 127.

[6] Matthew uses the traditional title 'the holy city' for Jerusalem (4.5; 27.53) but
probably only by way of convention. Cf. also 'the city of the great king' (5.35
quoting Ps. 47.3). The parallel passage in Jas. 5.12 has no mention of Jerusalem.

With Luke the case is different. In regard to the claims of Galilee and Jerusalem he pursues what may be called a policy of equation. We have seen it already applied to the question of the scene of the ministry (see above, p. 29); he also follows it out in other respects. If Galilee is 'holy' and the scene of revelation, so too is Jerusalem; if Jerusalem was the place where Jesus had been put to death, in Galilee also He had met with opposition, extending to attempts on His life (Luke 4.39). Luke certainly emphasized the importance of Jerusalem (cf. p. 30). In the early chapters it is regarded as almost the same as Israel itself (Luke 2.25, 35); note also the addition 'at Jerusalem' in the story of the transfiguration (Luke 9.31), and the specific mention of the 'siege' (21.20, 24) which is absent from the Matthean parallel (24). The mention of Jerusalem in Luke 24.47 may be an addition as it is out of construction, but there is no question of the genuineness of the divine command to tarry in the city in *v.* 49.

The absence of interest in the earthly life of Jesus and in the scene of His ministry was characteristic of the earliest apostolic preaching; such is the impression we derive from the first chapters of Acts. There is also little reference to what He had taught, though much teaching about Him. We must, however, in this matter allow for our lack of complete information. The urgency of their message made the apostles concentrate on the things that to them were most vital; but they did not neglect the careful and continuous instruction of converts (Acts 2.42), and it may be assumed that such instruction would include some account of the earthly life as well as of the teaching which Jesus had given. There is also significance in the casual statement that He went about doing good (Acts 10.36ff) and the reference to His miracles (Acts 2.22).[1]

This characteristic was continued in the missionary preaching of the Gospel, and the type of Christianity, mainly inspired by St Paul, which went forth to conquer the world seems to have neglected the actual teaching of Jesus and to have attached but little importance to the incidents of His life before the passion.[2]

---

[1] Dibelius suggests that 'examples' from the life of Jesus may have been used in the apostolic preaching (*From Tradition to Gospel*, p. 26).
[2] Cf. R. H. Lightfoot, *Hist. and Interpretation* etc., p. 210: 'In the gospel pro-

That St Paul's epistles should contain few references to the earthly life of Jesus is natural. He himself had received a direct revelation from the risen Lord and had no need of external events as a basis of his faith in Jesus (Gal. 1.15f). None the less St Paul attaches immense importance to the passion, resurrection, and the coming again. There is nothing in his ideas to suggest a non-historical theology such as that of the mystery religions. In the Epistle to the Hebrews there are more references to the earthly life than in all the Pauline epistles (e.g. 1.2f, 4.2; 8.1, 14; 9.28; 12.2f; 13.2f), but the emphasis is still laid on the sufferings, resurrection, and second coming.

As time went on and the return of the Lord was delayed, greater interest came to be taken in the earthly life and teaching (in Galilee perhaps it had never waned) and numerous accounts began to appear (cf. Luke 1.1) of which our Gospels are the sole survivors. But before continuous narratives were attempted there must have been a free circulation of sayings of Jesus and of stories, in a detached form, of events in His life. The delay in compiling fuller narratives is, however, in accord with Jewish ideas, for the Jews shewed little interest in comprehensive accounts of their teachers, though very careful to treasure their utterances, and to vague accounts of isolated incidents, especially if these could be turned to purposes of edification.[1] An interest in biography was characteristic of the Greeks and Romans and whoever wrote the first Gospel was definitely an innovator.

The earliest Gospel which we possess is Mark, but alongside it, and probably of much the same date, if not even earlier, there was another source or collection of sources, conventionally known as Q, which underlies the other two Synoptic Gospels. Although Mark records that teaching was constantly being given by Jesus he is primarily concerned with incidents; but in Matthew and Luke the teaching itself is given at some length, either from

claimed by St Paul it was not necessary, any more than in the creeds, to know any single event between the birth and passion of our Lord.' Dibelius, *From Tradition to Gospel*, p. 24, considered that the acts of Jesus 'had only an incidental and not an essential significance for the understanding of salvation'. The most striking utterance is that of Brunner who states that 'The Christian faith . . . is not interested in the "founder of Christianity" ' (*The Mediator*, p. 81).

[1] See Herbert Loewe in *The Transition from Judaism to Christianity*, I, p. 151. He also points out that there is no article on 'Biography' in the *Jewish Encyclopædia*.

Q or from other sources available to them. From passages assigned
to Q (though such attributions must be received with caution)
we should infer that 'the teaching of Jesus was ethical and eschatological rather than personal or Messianic'.[1] In contrast to this it
is to be remarked that the apostolic preaching as recorded in Acts
(apart from the somewhat obscure reference in 3.21) shews little
interest in eschatology. Eschatology was perhaps especially characteristic of Galilee where the hope of a divine intervention on
behalf of the nation had long been cherished.[2] Orthodox Judaism
was suspicious of apocalyptic forecasts; the rabbis, indeed,
ignored them and the considerable literature in which they were
contained.[3] Such literature, however, provides evidence of the
kind of ideas which were in circulation among the common
people.

In the fourth Gospel there is a different emphasis from that in
the Synoptists in regard to the earthly life of the Lord, though
its evidential value is recognized (e.g. in John 1.14 and the saying
in John 14.9: 'Have I been so long time with you, Philip, and
hast thou not known me?'; cf. also I John 4.2; II John 7). The
difference is in reality one of emphasis only, for as W. L. Knox
has said, 'The greatness of the Gospel (i.e. John) lies in the fact
that while it interprets the life of Jesus in terms of the theology of
the age, it never loses sight of the concrete historical figure of
the synoptic tradition. . . . There are moments when it comes
dangerously near to presenting Jesus as a purely docetic epiphany
on the stage of history, but these are always corrected by the
evangelist's fidelity to the main Christian tradition' (*Some Hellenistic Elements*, etc., pp. 89f). That the writer of the fourth Gospel
knew the Synoptics, or something very like them, is highly
probable, for at times he seems deliberately to correct or supplement them. In particular he goes out of his way (as we have
seen) to draw attention to the importance of Jerusalem in the
ministry of Jesus; but this by no means implies an anti-Galilean
attitude. There is, of course, the statement that no prophet can
come out of Galilee (John 7.52); but it is placed on the lips of

[1] Kirsopp Lake in *The Beginnings of Christianity*, V, p. 11.
[2] Lagrange, *Saint Marc*, p. 118, thinks that the Galileans were ever anxious to
bring in the kingdom by force and that the parable in Mark 4.26-9 was intended to
teach them patience: cf. Jas. 5.8.
[3] See G. F. Moore, *Judaism*, I, pp. 127ff.

Pharisees and its obvious inconsistency with the O.T.[1] carries its own condemnation.[2]

It is over the post-resurrection appearances of Jesus that the clash of tradition between Galilee and Jerusalem is most striking, and even startling. Before considering them in detail, however, some general comments may be made. In Mark and Matthew the fact of the empty tomb is taken for granted, but Luke offers evidence for it, whilst John has links with both traditions. For Mark and Matthew the importance of the resurrection is mainly preparatory, but for Luke it is the crown of the work of Jesus. John has certain resemblances to Luke, but for him also the ascension is the culminating point. Mark records no 'appearance', and points forward to the parousia, while Matthew tells of the appearance to the women at the tomb, which so far as it goes supports Jerusalem as the scene of such manifestations.[3]

The various narratives of the appearances of Jesus after He had risen from the dead cannot easily be reconciled and no attempt has apparently been made by the evangelists to do so.[4] Matthew specifically declares that the Lord appeared in Galilee (Matt. 28.16ff; cf. 26.32), and though Mark, apart from the 'ending', is not so definite, such appearances can be inferred from 14.28; 16.7.[5] St Paul apparently knew of at least one appearance in Galilee (I Cor. 15.6), which may be the same as that in Matt. 28.16f, though the order in which he records the revelations of the risen Lord is uncertain. Luke 24 and John 20, on the other hand, confine the appearances to Jerusalem and its neighbourhood. In view of the distance between Jerusalem and Galilee (a journey of three days)[6] and the brief compass of time within which the appearances are said to have taken place, it is impossible to fit

---

[1] The exact birth-place of the Northern prophets is not always certain: Deborah came from Galilee, and perhaps Elisha and Hosea. The tomb of Jonah is shewn at Neby-Junis, near Nazareth, and that of Nahum not far from Capernaum. The latter is a very late tradition: see J. M. Powis Smith in *I.C.C.*, p. 286, who concludes that there is no indication of Nahum's Galilean origin.

[2] The reference, however, may be to the contemporary state of the land: 'Is Galilee the sort of place from which a prophet would arise nowadays?'

[3] See R. H. Lightfoot, *Locality and Doctrine* etc., pp. 95ff.

[4] For a fuller discussion see E. G. Selwyn in *Essays Catholic and Critical*, pp. 291-314, P. Gardner Smith, *The Narratives of the Resurrection*, and A. M. Ramsey, *The Resurrection of Christ*.

[5] It has been suggested that the ending of Mark was deliberately suppressed because of its conflict with the tradition represented by Luke and John.

[6] Dalman, *Sacred Sites* etc., p. 209.

the various accounts into one another or even to accept them as they stand, though more complete knowledge might enable us to do so. This fact, it may be pointed out, is a testimony to the candour of the writers and by no means takes away from the value of their evidence as to the historical truth of the central event.

In the account of the post-resurrection appearances in John 20, Galilee is ignored; but in Chapter 21 there is a narrative told in some detail, of such an appearance. The narrative has, in its general outlook, close affinities with the point of view of Mark and Matthew, for not only is it concerned with Galilee, but it exhibits no desire to adduce any proof of the reality of the resurrection, it is interested in the mission and leadership of the Church, and it looks forward beyond the resurrection. On the value of this narrative critics are strongly divided.[1] Bacon, Strachan, and Spitta, for example, allocate it to an editor; Stanton to a different member of the group who were responsible for the rest of the Gospel; while Harnack accepts it as an original part of the Gospel, possibly based on the lost ending of Mark.[2] In spite of similarities in style with the rest of John the apparent duplication of the story told in Luke 5.1ff concerning a much earlier period, is bound to raise suspicion. It is also possible to separate the dialogue in John 21. 15-23 from its supposed setting in Galilee, and it may be that this setting was supplied by an editor who wished to reconcile the Galilean and Jerusalem traditions.[3]

In confining the post-resurrection appearances to Jerusalem John 20 finds what might be regarded as unexpected support from Luke, who here goes against his fellow Synoptists.[4] It is, however, probable that he had a separate source for the narratives of the passion and resurrection,[5] and that the 'bias' against Galilee may come from it.

[1] See Hoskyns, *The Fourth Gospel*, pp. 550f.

[2] R. H. Lightfoot, *op. cit.*, p. 102, also considers that it is 'an integral part of the fourth Gospel'. Loofs, *Die Auferstehungsberichte und ihr Wert*, pp. 31f, thought that a post-resurrection story of an appearance to Peter (though not in Galilee) has been combined with a pre-resurrection narrative.

[3] In this connexion it may be worth noticing that Alexander Schweitzer in *Das Evangelium Johannis* (1841) suggested that John is the result of the combination of a short Jerusalem gospel with a Galilean life of Jesus.

[4] Mark 16.20 suggests that the eleven went forth from Jerusalem and thus seems to support the 'Jerusalem' tradition: see Taylor, *St Mark*, p. 613.

[5] See A. M. Perry, *The Sources of Luke's Passion Narrative*.

As it seems impossible to reconcile the two traditions most critics decide for one or other of them. Burkitt rejected the Galilean tradition because he considered that had it been true the centre of Christianity would have remained there and not have been transferred to Jerusalem.[1] He accepted the Lucan view that St Peter and the apostles never went more than a day's journey from Jerusalem, and even suggested (most improbably) that the well-known *Quo vadis?* legend really belonged to Easter Day. In a letter to Kirsopp Lake he pointed out that Mark 14.28 'Howbeit, after I am raised up, I will go before you into Galilee' is omitted by the third century Fayyum fragment (Pap. Rainer I.53ff), but he admitted that it was probably due to carelessness, and that the verse was an original part of the Gospel, and not an insertion following Mark 16.7 and the Galilean tradition. J. Weiss thought it unlikely that the disciples would have fled as far as Galilee,[2] and suggested that the appearances there were intended to provide a fulfilment of the prediction of Jesus that the kingdom would be brought in by His death, and that a triumphant return to Galilee would follow.[3] Many critics, however, accept the Galilean tradition (so Streeter, *The Four Gospels*, pp. 351ff), though the more advanced do so on the grounds that, since the whole resurrection story was based on an illusion, it was more natural to suppose that it had originated amidst the scenes of the former activity of Jesus.[4] Others prefer it owing to the difficulty of accounting for its invention; an argument which can be met on the supposition that the Galileans created the legend to support their own prestige against Jerusalem, though the exact opposite is more probable.

Scholars have gone to extraordinary lengths in their efforts to reconcile the different accounts, some even suggest that there have been mistakes in identifying the sites. The most perverse of this kind of suggestion must surely be that of Noack who began

---

[1] *Christian Beginnings*, pp. 76ff.

[2] The flight to Galilee is mentioned in the *Gospel of Peter* (in James, *The Apocryphal N.T.*, p. 94).

[3] Reference to the theory of a return to Galilee was made above, p. 35. For an examination of the views of Burkitt and of Weiss see Kirsopp Lake, *op. cit.*, V, pp. 7-16.

[4] Goguel holds that it was in Galilee that the belief in the resurrection had its birth and that the Christophanies were later transferred to Jerusalem: see *L'Église Primitive*, p. 23, *La foi à la Résurrection* etc., pp. 310ff.

Die Geschichte Jesu (1876) by declaring that: 'It is in the Galilean district which forms the scene of the Song of Solomon that the reader of this book must be prepared to find the Golgotha of the Cross;' he went still further and claimed that the pre-exilic Jerusalem was located in Coele-Syria. But such attempts to find novel sites for historical events go back very early, at least to the period following the recognition of Christianity by the Roman Empire and the swarms of pilgrims who then paid visits to Palestine. Supposed 'Galilean' sites were located near Jerusalem—not it may be inferred from any feeling of jealousy between Jerusalem and Galilee, but from that cupidity which multiplies objects of interest to draw revenue from the visitor. In the sixth century 'Galilee' itself could be found on the Mount of Olives[1]. This identification persisted, and was known to Saewulf who visited Jerusalem in 1102, and to Sir John Maundeville two centuries later. Galilee for its part tried to 'cash in' on the tourist trade and discovered various sites in its own locality; the scene of the birth of Jesus, for example, was placed at Bethlehem in Zebulon, some dozen miles north of Nazareth.

---

[1] *Brev. de Hieros.* in Geyer, *Itinera*, p. 155. See further R. Hoffman, *Galilaea auf dem Oelberg.*

IV

THE CHURCH IN GALILEE

The only definite mention of Christianity in Galilee in the book of the Acts is the statement in Acts 9.31 that the Church[1] throughout Judaea, Galilee, and Samaria had rest after the conversion of Saul. In Acts 8.1 it had been said that in consequence of the persecution which followed the death of Stephen many Christians from Jerusalem fled to Judaea and Samaria. Though Galilee is not here mentioned it should probably be included as an obvious place of refuge, for St Luke, as we have already seen (see above, p. 29), often gave an inclusive meaning to Judaea. In so doing he merely adopted a common practice found also in classical writers, for when the kingdom of Herod Agrippa became a procuratorial district it was often referred to as Judaea, although it included Samaria and parts of Galilee.[2]

St Paul on his way to Damascus probably passed through Galilee, but we are not informed that he took any measures against the Christians; no doubt he was anxious to reach his destination as soon as possible. W. L. Knox suggested that as Galilee was then under Herod Antipas his activities would be limited, and that in any case the authority of the Sanhedrin there would be practically non-existent (*St Paul and the Church at Jerusalem*, pp. 45, 66). That Christians in Galilee were molested seems certain; otherwise the statement in Acts 9.31 would be meaningless. Some may have fled before the storm, to return when the tide of persecution had ebbed.

Damascus was closely linked with Galilee. Cut off from the west and north by high mountain ranges and having only the desert to the east it naturally looked towards Palestine with which,

---

[1] Some inferior MSS, the Old Latin, some Vulgate MSS, Syr. Harcl. read 'churches' and thus attribute a 'church' to Galilee.
[2] So Tacitus *Annales* xii.23, *Hist*. v.9, Suetonius *Claudius* xxviii. Similar indefiniteness is found in regard to Galatia and in modern times Calabria covers a very different area from its namesake in earlier days.

moreover, it was connected by great highways; Pliny counted it among the cities of the Decapolis (*Hist. Nat.* v.16). It is probable therefore that the Gospel was brought to Damascus by Christians from Galilee, though the suggestion of W. Grundmann in *Z.N.T.W.*, 1939, p. 46, that it was evangelized by the brethren of the Lord, is pure surmise, and some Galileans may at this time have fled thither. At any rate the city must have had a considerable number of Christians in it, otherwise there would have been no point in Saul's expedition.[1] Damascus was well suited to give a welcome to the new teaching, for it had a large Jewish population and proselytes to Judaism had been made among the women of the city (Josephus *Bell. Jud.* II.xx.2). Synagogues are mentioned in Acts 9.2 and 20, and Ananias had a good reputation with the Jews (Acts 22.12). There was or had been in Damascus the so-called Zadokite community which had fled thither from Jerusalem in order to gain greater freedom.[2] Among the members of such a community the Gospel might spread more easily than among Jews of stricter orthodoxy.

Direct evidence concerning the Church in Galilee before the events leading to the fall of Jerusalem in A.D. 70 is thus very scanty. Possibly accounts of the Jewish Christians there may have been suppressed at a later time,[3] or, what is more probable, interest in them having lapsed no one was at pains to preserve such notices, at least in the Church at large. Burkitt suggested that Luke in the early chapters of Acts may have made use of an account of the Church in Palestine compiled by Mark (*Christian Beginnings*, p. 83). This suggestion seems to me to be more ingenious than probable. More certain evidence is to be found in

---

[1] Some of them were probably fugitives from the persecution which had arisen over Stephen, though no mention of Damascus is made in Acts 11.19.

[2] See further Charles in *Apoc. and Pseudepig. of O.T.*, II., pp. 785ff. Margoliouth *Expositor* (1911) pp. 499ff (1912) pp. 213ff maintained that the community itself was Christian. In the opinion of many scholars the recently discovered Dead Sea Scrolls came from it. See H. H. Rowley *The Zadokite Fragments and the Dead Sea Scrolls* (1952).

[3] Such suppressions seem to have taken place many times in the long history of the Church, especially where heretical, or supposedly heretical, views have been suspected. This may account for the absence of information concerning the early history of the Church in Egypt (see Elliott-Binns, *The Beginnings of Western Christendom*, p. 129; cf. p. 90). One of the most interesting efforts at suppression (fortunately it was unsuccessful) was the endeavour to destroy all the early accounts of the life of St Francis when St Bonaventura had put forth the official account (see Elliott-Binns, *The Decline and Fall of the Medieval Papacy*, p. 97 note 103).

the sources which lie behind the Synoptic Gospels. In Mark,[1] in Q, and perhaps especially in passages peculiar to Matthew, we may find matter which reflects the special interests of Galilean Christians, and its very preservation may have been due to their care. Most valuable of all, however, is the canonical writing known as the Epistle of St James.[2]

Since there are differences of opinion as to the date and place of origin of this epistle it will be necessary to discuss these points before making use of it in this connexion.

Various suggestions as to the place of origin of the epistle have been made. Streeter, who accepted its use by I Clement and in *The Shepherd* of Hermas (cf. p. 47, note 2), went as far afield as Rome (*The Primitive Church*, pp. 189ff); whilst Von Soden, Brückner, and more recently S. G. F. Brandon, think that it may have been written in Alexandria by refugees from Jerusalem after the fall of the city in A.D. 70.[3] The great majority of critics, however, prefer a Syrian or Palestinian location. Antioch is favoured by many[4]; but this seems an unlikely place of origin, for had the epistle been connected with the church in such an important city it would surely never have been allowed to fall into neglect as was James. Those who accept the traditional authorship find in Jerusalem the obvious place of origin. Against this it may be said that there is nothing in the epistle which suggests the conditions prevailing there and its whole outlook seems freer and less ecclesiastical than one would have supposed to be natural in a writing coming from the mother church of Christendom. The background seems to be rural rather than urban and, as Deissmann has said, 'The Epistle of James will be best understood in the open-air, beside the piled sheaves of the harvest' (*Light from the Ancient East*, p. 248). Ropes ('St James' in *I.C.C.*, p. 49) favoured some town in Palestine, possibly Caesarea.[5] There are strong similarities with the background of the Synoptic Gospels

[1] In *The Sources of the Second Gospel* it is argued by A. T. Cadoux that a Palestinian gospel, perhaps derived from St Peter and written in Aramaic, was incorporated in Mark.

[2] Schoeps, *Theologie und Geschichte des Judenchristentums*, pp. 343ff, regards the epistle as the work of a catholic Jewish Christian writing in early post-apostolic times.

[3] The fact that the readers depended on rainfall (5.7) and not irrigation seems to rule this out.

[4] E.g. J. Weiss, *Das Urchristentum*, p. 578 note 1, Goodspeed, *Int. to N.T.*, pp. 291f, and Hort, *The Epistle of St James*, pp. xxiiif.

[5] G. Kittel also favours Palestine; see *Z.N.T.W.* (1942), pp. 71-105.

and these point to a Galilean origin. But the brevity of the
writing and the absence of direct statements make it difficult to
reach any certain conclusion in the matter, though after much
thought on the question I am persuaded that Galilee best fits the
situation.

As different scholars have suggested various places of origin,
so have they favoured various dates for James.[1] Many regard it
as a late composition, others place it very early, whilst a third
group, although they accept the authorship of James, put it
towards the close of his life. Lechler, *Post-Apostolic Times*, I, pp.
291f regarded it as exceedingly early and as coming from the
time before the Gospel had spread outside Palestine and even
before the death of St Stephen.[2]

Recent critics on the whole have favoured an early date. The
most careful and detailed examination is that of G. Kittel in
Z.N.T.W. (1942) pp. 71-105, and at the end of it he decides that
it is the earliest of all Christian documents.

Those who favour a late date explain its apparent primitiveness
and undogmatic (some call it anti-dogmatic) tone as due to 'the
moralistic tendencies (which) emerged in certain circles of
Christianity towards the opening of the second century'.[3] In my
judgement, however, it seems more easy to suppose that it
represents the outlook of the earliest days, before there had been
time to consider the theological consequences of accepting Jesus
as the Messiah and Son of God, or its effects in relation to the
Jewish community; a time, it may be, when there was still strong
hope that the nation at large might accept His claims. Windisch
in his commentary finds in the epistle a piety which is based on
the Law, but on the Law as purified by the teaching of Jesus,
and concludes that it represents a Christianity common in the
apostolic period which is unaffected by Jerusalem or Pauline
influences.[4] The Calvinist Marty also holds that the epistle comes
from surroundings in which the evangelical tradition has been
preserved in its primitive simplicity.[5] This primitive simplicity

---

[1] See Moffatt, *Int. to the Literature of the N.T.* (1918), pp. 468ff.

[2] He quotes with approval the opinion of Mangold that it represented 'the
simplest expression of Christian consciousness, still untouched by complex dogmatic
reflexions, as it must have developed with original freshness in the circle of Jews
that believed in the Messiah'.   [3] Moffatt, *op. cit.*, p. 471.

[4] In *Handbuch zum N.T.* (1911), pp. 21 and 36.

[5] *L'Épître de Jacques* (1935), pp. 28of.

might, however, have been preserved at a fairly late date in circles away from the main stream of development. Jean Réville found in James, as also in *The Shepherd* and the *Didache*, traces of a popular faith which was fundamentally moral and uninterested in speculation, and one which went back to the Gospel as taught by Jesus in Galilee.[1]

The primitive simplicity of James, although it may conceivably be explained as due to some kind of 'fossil' preservation, is surely most easily to be attributed to the early date of the epistle itself, especially as other tokens of early date are not lacking. Among them are the absence of warnings against false teaching; the mention of 'the kingdom' (2.5), so central in the Synoptic Gospels, but finding little place in other N.T. writings and being virtually absent from the fourth Gospel (but cf. John 3.3, 5); and the expectation of the parousia (5.7). Furthermore, although the epistle is full of reminiscences of the sayings of Jesus as contained in the Synoptists, there is seldom verbal agreement, a circumstance which strongly suggests that they come from a period before the sayings had become stereotyped in a literary form.

So far as I know all those who accept an early date for the epistle accept also the attribution to James, the brother of the Lord, as set out in the ascription. This ascription I am unable to regard as original. In the first place it seems most unsuitable as a description of the contents of the writing, for it presupposes something on an ecumenical scale; instead we have teaching apparently addressed to the needs of a single community. Again the whole atmosphere is different from that which we should associate with James and the church at Jerusalem. Moreover the history of the circulation of the epistle raises difficulties. It may have been current in Rome at the end of the first and the beginning of the second century,[2] but does not seem to have been regarded as possessing any special authority. The first writer to attribute it to James is Origen who is also the first to make much use of it. Had it been recognized as by James its history would surely have been very different; for his position as head of the

---

[1] *La valeur du témoignage hist. du 'Pasteur' d'Hermas* (1900), p. 14.
[2] Ropes, *op. cit.*, pp. 86ff, denies that it was known to 1 Clem. or Hermas or to other Christian writers before Origen.

mother church at Jerusalem and his reputation as a saint and martyr would have given it great prestige and its use and circulation would have been continuous. But if it lacked the authority of a great name and the support of an important church the neglect which it suffered is easily explained as due to its defective Christology and other omissions. It was, one may suppose, involved in the general fate of Jewish Christianity.

The ascription was probably prefixed about the middle of the second century. Harnack considered that there was at that time a widespread movement to give apostolic authorship to all anonymous writings.[1] Streeter thought that the attribution was the work of an Alexandrian scribe (*The Primitive Church*, p. 191). My own opinion is that it was part of a general campaign in certain Jewish Christian and Ebionite quarters to exalt St James at the expense of St Peter,[2] evidence of which can be found in the sources lying behind the Clementine romances,[3] and also in the *Gospel according to the Hebrews*.[4] Its subsequent popularity can thus be accounted for, as the attribution to St James would give it a new lease of life in the Catholic Church whilst Jewish Christians (including those who are classed as Ebionites)[5] would hold it in special regard.

We are now in a position to endeavour to conjecture what were the beliefs of the early Christians in Galilee. Dibelius (*From Tradition to Gospel*, p. 29) recognizes a type of primitive Christianity whose characteristics were: (*a*) an emphasis on the teaching of Jesus; (*b*) an undeveloped Christology; (*c*) an absence of any doctrine of redemption; and (*d*) a desire to maintain close links with Judaism. He speaks of it as a 'sort of Christianity' which is

---

[1] *Lehre der Zwölf Apostel* (in *Texte und Untersuchungen, ii*), pp. 106ff.

[2] Gore thought that the tendency of Jewish Christians to exalt St James goes much further back and that the special emphasis on the position of St Peter in Matthew was intended as a corrective (*The Holy Spirit and the Church*, p. 51).

[3] See below, pp. 52f.

[4] Goguel *La Naissance du Christianisme*, p. 57, explained the account of the appearance to St James which it describes as an elaboration of I Cor. 15.7 *ad majorem Jacobi gloriam* by those who upheld what he calls 'dynastic' Christianity.

[5] Schoeps in *Theol. und Geschichte des Judenchristentums* tries to shew that the teaching of the Ebionites represented that of the first Jewish Christians (see further his notes in *J.T.S.*, N.S., IV, pp. 219ff), Marcel Simon, however, thinks that Ebionism was far more diverse and complex than Schoeps supposes, and that, as revealed in the Clementine romances, it was more deeply rooted in heterodox Judaism. He also doubts whether *The Preaching of Peter* which lies behind them represents Jewish Christianity in general or any coherent Ebionite system. See *Journal of Ecclesiastical Hist.*, I, pp. 114ff.

really Judasim without Jewish national limitations, and which 'brought over a large amount of Jewish prayers, hymns, and exhortations into the Christian Church'. This type of Christianity is very like that which is represented in the Epistle of James.

(*a*) The writer is certainly interested in the teaching of Jesus, but shews little interest in teaching about Him. He seems unconcerned about the events of His earthly life,[1] and there is a strange failure to appeal to His example, an appeal which is so frequent in other N.T. epistles and is considered by Dodd, *Gospel and Law*, pp. 39ff, to have been characteristic of early Christianity. When he wishes to adduce an example of patience he refers to the prophets and to Job (Jas. 5.10f; cf. Heb. 12.2) and when he requires an instance of prevailing prayer it is to Elijah that he turns (Jas. 5.17; cf. Heb. 5.7). He makes no mention of the resurrection, though the notice of the parousia (Jas. 5.7) might presuppose it.[2]

(*b*) When compared with other N.T. writings, save perhaps the early chapters of Acts, the Christology is unelaborated, if not defective. The reference to 'our Lord Jesus Christ, the glory' (Jas. 2.1) is too obscure to throw light on his views.

(*c*) Whilst the writer believes in the forgiveness of sins (5.15f, 20) he does not connect it with any doctrine of redemption or atonement. Here again there is a parallel with the early chapters of Acts where no special doctrinal significance is attached to the death of Christ.[3] Schoeps suggests that for Jewish Christians it was valued as evidence of His humanity.[4]

(*d*) The general tone of the epistle reveals a close approximation to Judaism and the O.T., so much so that some critics look upon it as originally a Jewish document which has received Christian interpolations.[5] It may, indeed, have been addressed to Jews in general,

---

[1] This may seem strange in a Galilean document, but can be explained by the early date and the urgency of the general message; cf. pp. 36f above.

[2] Mark looks upon the parousia as the culmination of the resurrection; see R. H. Lightfoot, *Locality and Doctrine* etc., p. 63.

[3] Cf. B. S. Easton, *Early Christianity*, pp. 85ff.

[4] *Op. cit.*, p. 76. Schoeps considers that the Christology of the Ebionites was 'Adoptionist' and that they attached no doctrinal importance to the death of Jesus; to them He was a second Moses—is Heb. 3.1ff intended to combat such an idea?—the giver of a new and perfect law, and also the Messiah who will return in glory.

[5] So Spitta, *Der Brief des Jakobus* (1896), and L. Massebieau, 'L'Épître de Jacques est-elle l'œuvre d'un Chrétien?' in *Rev. de l'Hist. des Rel.* (1895). Similar views have been advanced by J. Halévy in *Rev. Sem.*, 1914, pp. 249ff, and in the eccentric work of Arnold Meyer which forms an additional volume of *Z.N.T.W.*, 1930.

and not merely to Christian Jews, though this is improbable.

If, however, the epistle was addressed to non-Christian Jews, as well as believers, it might have been considered advisable to preserve some reticence over specific Christian teaching. As to omissions in general it need hardly be pointed out that the epistle is not a lengthy document and that its readers would be presumed to have some knowledge already. Much would therefore be taken for granted. There are many cases of similar omissions in other N.T. epistles, presumably for this very reason.

In considering the doctrinal views of the early Jewish Christians it would be a grave mistake to suppose that they followed a single pattern. Intellectually all was in a state of flux, or perhaps it would be more accurate to say that the implications of the faith, even of Christology, had not yet been faced. It must be remembered that the Jews had never valued 'orthodoxy' of belief as Christianity would later value it, and we must therefore guard against reading back into primitive times attitudes which belong to a later period.

In our Lord's day the Jewish Church included Pharisees, Sadducees and Essenes, between whom there were very wide differences of belief. The rabbis subsequently tried to minimize such differences and Josephus already takes the same line.[1] The bond which held the Jewish community together was ethical and not doctrinal; Judaism, it has been said, was 'not a system and never had a creed'.[2] With the Pharisees moral theology (*Halachah*) was fixed, but not expository or doctrinal theology (*Haggadah*). The latter is the free expression of the opinions of various rabbis and might include views which were different and even contradictory.[3] There was thus great freedom of expression and little danger of accusations of heresy. 'It is remarkable how Jewish theology, owing to its lack of system, was able, as it were, to dabble in ideas without getting into trouble.'[4]

The suggestion has recently been put forward by P. Carrington in *The Primitive Christian Catechism* (1940), and elaborated by E. G. Selwyn in *The First Epistle of St Peter*, that there existed an

---

[1] Cf. Lietzmann, *The Beginnings of the Christian Church*, p. 43.
[2] Herford, *The Pharisees*, p. 13.
[3] Cf. the diverse and inconsistent views expressed in II Baruch and IV Ezra; see Charles, *The Apocalypse of Baruch*, pp. lxix-lxxi.
[4] Montefiore, *Rabbinic Literature and Gospel Teachings*, p. 25.

outline of teaching which lies behind many of the epistles. A good
case seems to have been made out for the theory, which incidentally had been suggested by A. Seeberg in *Der Katechismus der
Urchristenheit* (1903), though the evidence is not exactly com-
pelling. In their various tables of the contents of the suggested
outline both scholars include passages from James. These passages, however, do not fit into the outline nearly so well as other
material derived mainly from the Pauline epistles and I Peter. I
have done much work on the question as to whether, and to
what extent, James was dependent on such an outline, and so
far have been unable to reach any definite conclusion, but I in-
cline to the view that if James used an outline it was not exactly
that which lies behind the other N.T. writers. Such outlines
probably go back to Jewish examples,[1] and he may have had
before him a form which was later modified and expanded to
meet the special needs of Gentile Christians. No information as
to the views of the early Jewish Christians can therefore be derived from the later and more elaborate catechetical material; all
that we can safely accept is what is contained in James.

Of the organization of Christians in Galilee in the earliest days
we have little definite knowledge.[2] W. L. Knox in *St Paul and
the Church at Jerusalem* put forward the view that for some time
the church at Jerusalem was the sole organized Christian community, though there might be isolated Christians in Galilee
(pp. 1 and 7). The organization of the Church in other areas was
the result of the mission preaching of the Twelve[3] and others
who were sent out from Jerusalem (p. 78). He thought further
that in Jerusalem alone were there celebrations of the Eucharist
and that Jewish Christians from elsewhere would only be able to
partake of it when they came up to the capital (p. 85). Many
Galileans, he considered, remained in Jerusalem until the Church
had been organized in their own localities (p. 89).

With this picture of the state of Christianity in its primitive
days I cannot entirely agree. If, as I believe, the Epistle of James

---

[1] They may have received the sanction of Jesus Himself, for when the disciples
were sent forth to prepare the way for Him some kind of teaching outline may well
have been given to them; probably only in an oral form.

[2] For Ebionitic organization which may have developed from that of the first
Jewish Christians, see Schoeps, *op. cit.*, pp. 289ff.

[3] Streeter, *The Four Gospels*, p. 233, thought that some of the Twelve returned to
Galilee.

is very early and comes from Galilee,[1] we find that Christians there had their own synagogue (Jas. 2.2) and also their own elders of the Church (5.14). They seem not yet to have had any elaborate organization for the care from common funds of needy brethren, these were still dependent on the spontaneous charity of individual Christians (Jas. 2.15f; cf. Rom. 12.13; I Cor. 16.15f), which was hardly the case in Jerusalem if we can trust the accounts in the early chapters of Acts. The community contained both rich and poor, though we need not suppose that all the rich men who were denounced were believers. In spite of some disputing (Jas. 3.14; 4.1f, 11) there was a strong feeling of fellowship among them, as can be inferred from their praying for one another and in the mutual confession of sins (5.16). As to Knox's idea that the Eucharist was celebrated only in Jerusalem, one may ask 'Was it at this early date so formal a thing, and may it not have been something very simple, and even the accompaniment of every meal?'[2]

The possession of a synagogue and elders of their own need not imply that Jewish Christians had at this date entirely severed relations with Judaism. Many seem to have combined both allegiances, and even to have observed the Jewish Sabbath as well as the Lord's day.[3] It is also probable that some at least still took part in the temple worship at the great festivals.[4] The saying of Christ in Matt. 5.23f is strong evidence that Christians made their offerings at the altar,[5] and the narrative of St Peter and the half-shekel (Matt. 17.24ff) suggests that they continued to pay the temple tax, for otherwise there would have been little point in recording the incident.

ADDITIONAL NOTE: THE CLEMENTINE ROMANCES

The value of the Clementine Romances has been very variously assessed by different scholars. Schoeps, who rates them highly, in *The Journal of Eccles. Hist.* III, p. 103, quoted with approval

---

[1] This argument, of course, falls to the ground if James is late, or, as some scholars suppose, was itself a product of the Church in Jerusalem.

[2] See Elliott-Binns, *The Beginnings of Western Christendom*, pp. 367ff.

[3] See *The Apost. Constitutions* vii.23 and Eusebius *Hist. Eccles.* III.xxvii.5; also Schoeps, *op. cit.*, p. 144.

[4] Cf. Acts 2.46; 3.1; 5.12, 20, 42—and even as late as 21.23f. Taylor, *The Life and Ministry* etc., pp. 204f, thinks that the sayings in Mark 14.58; Matt. 26.61 'may reflect a certain uneasiness on the part of the Jewish disciples who continued to observe the practice of Temple worship'.   [5] So J. Weiss, *Urchristentum*, p. 39.

from Heinrich Weinel's memorial address in honour of R. A.
Lipsius delivered in 1920 that 'The value of the Pseudo-Clemen-
tine writings in particular for the history of early Christianity will
assuredly one day again be rated more highly, when someone
ventures anew into this portion of the "virgin forest".' On the
other hand E. Schwartz in *Z.N.T.W.*, 1931, pp. 151-99, concluded that they were pure romances without any real significance
for the history of early Jewish Christianity.

In attempting to assess their value much will depend on the
view taken as to their date and origin. This is a very obscure
question on which much material will be found in O. Cullmann,
Le Problème littéraire et historique du Roman Pseudo-Clémentin, as
well as in Schoeps' great work. Streeter (*The Four Gospels*, p. 258
note) dated the *Homilies* c. 180, but most scholars would bring it
down much later; so too Rendall, *The Epistle of St James and
Judaic Christianity*, pp. 133ff, dated the *Letter to James* about the
same period. But though in their present form the romances are
comparatively late there can be little doubt that they depend on
much earlier sources, such as the *Preaching of Peter*, and probably
had their origin in Jewish Christian circles in the Transjordan
region in the second century, which may have preserved memories
and traditions handed down by the fugitives from the Jewish War.

The Clementine Romances, as already pointed out, shew great
interest in St James and are at pains to exalt his position. This
also is evidence for the date and origin, if not of the writings
themselves, at least for the sources lying behind them, for in the
latter half of the second century there was a general, or possibly
Jewish Christian, interest in the brother of the Lord. This can be
seen from the numerous legends which were being circulated
about him, such as those related by Hegesippus (cf. Eusebius
II.xxiii), that in the *Gospel according to the Hebrews*, and others in
various apocryphal gospels (see Index to M. R. James, *The
Apocryphal N.T.*). There were also numerous works attributed to
him such as the *Protevangelium Jacobi* which, since it is quoted by
Origen, must go back to the second century, and the *Ascents of
James*, an Ebionite work quoted by Epiphanius *Haer.* xxx.16,
and possibly used by Hegesippus (cf. Lightfoot, *Galatians*, p.
367, note 1). There were also other works attributed to him
which have been lost or are of much later date.

V

JERUSALEM AND THE TWELVE

THE transfer of the centre of the Church from Galilee to Jerusalem was followed soon after by changes in the government and administration of the Church in Jerusalem itself. In the days immediately succeeding the ascension the twelve apostles enjoyed great prestige and their number was completed after the falling away of Judas (Acts i.15ff).[1] In the eyes of St Luke and in later tradition the number itself was significant.[2] The apostles corresponded to the twelve princes over the various tribes mentioned in Num. 1.44 etc., and were to be the future rulers of the Kingdom (Matt. 19.27ff; Luke 22.28, 30).[3] In the early chapters of Acts they held a high, and indeed, a unique position (Acts 2.42f; 4.33ff; 5.12ff; 6.2ff; 8.1; 11.1), and even at a later date the Pauline school admitted that the Church was founded upon them (Eph. 2.20). It may be that they alone are represented as having received the Holy Spirit and tongues of fire at Pentecost.[4] But they possessed no despotic authority, and their primary function seems to have been to bear witness to the resurrection (Acts 1.22; 2.32; 3.15).

That Jesus selected certain of His followers to be near Him and that much of the later part of His ministry was devoted to their training seems beyond reasonable doubt. What is not so certain is that they were twelve in number, or that they formed

---

[1] Dodd suggests that the place of Judas was filled up because he was an apostate and that no further elections were made as it was assumed that the Twelve, even if no longer alive, would be the rulers of the new Israel (*According to the Scriptures*, p. 58 note 1).

[2] *Clem. Recog.* iv.35 compared them to the twelve months of the year and claimed that a thirteenth was unthinkable. This, it may be, was directed against St Paul.

[3] At this time Judas was one of the Twelve and the evangelists would appear to include him among the rulers so designated.

[4] So Hamilton, *The People of God*, II, pp. 211ff, has argued. Gore thought that the Spirit was given to the whole body of the disciples. He attaches special importance to Acts 2.17f (*The Holy Spirit and the Church*, p. 12).

a kind of permanent 'college' apart from the rest.[1] The mission entrusted to them in Galilee (Mark 3.15) may have been temporary only. Vincent Taylor thinks that when Mark was written they had become little more than a memory.[2] It is certainly strange that if they had been a distinct and definite body its exact composition should have been forgotten within the lifetime of those who had known Jesus. That such was the case seems to be implied by the variety in the lists of the names of those who were supposed to have been of the number of the Twelve (cf. Mark 3.13ff; Matt. 2.2-4; Luke 6.12ff; Acts 1.13). That they were thought of by Mark as distinct from the rest of the disciples is clear (2.15); so clear, indeed, that Ed. Meyer thought that a 'twelve' source was used by him. If ever the 'Twelve' formed a separate body we know little of their subsequent history,[3] save for the three, Peter, James, and John, who formed a kind of inner circle during the lifetime of the Master. The silence of the N.T. writers suggests that they were not interested in them; which may mean that none of them, save Peter and John, was in any way connected with a prominent Church. Had they been so connected we may be sure that records concerning them would have been preserved. The violent death of James, the brother of John, led to the withdrawal of St Peter (Acts 12.1ff)[4] and probably to the flight of such others of the Twelve as were still in Jerusalem.

Later legends tell us that the Twelve remained in Jerusalem for twelve years and then dispersed to the ends of the earth.[5] Such a wide dispersal seems improbable, and it is much more

[1] Fairbairn had 'no doubt that Christ appointed twelve Apostles, that the number twelve bore an ideal significance, and that they had certain specific and defined functions', but he rejected 'any theory of the corporate being and authority of a defined Apostolical body' (*The Place of Christ in Modern Theology* pp. 531f).

[2] *St Mark*, p. 202; cf. p. 229 and the long note 'The Twelve and the Apostles', pp. 619ff.

[3] 'What became of the twelve apostles is one of the mysteries of history' (Streeter, *The Four Gospels*, p. 232).

[4] Foakes Jackson and Kirsopp Lake, *The Beginnings of Christianity*, II, pp. 156f, think that Acts 12.1-17 should follow 9.31 and that St Peter then made his Palestinian tour described in 9.31ff.

[5] It is stated in Eusebius, *op. cit.*, III.v.2, that the apostles were banished from the whole land of Judaea through plots against them and so they went forth to the ends of the earth. In III.vii.8 it is said that the greater number of the apostles and disciples, with James himself, lived in Jerusalem being 'that place's most sure bulwark' (ἕρκος ὥσπερ ὀχυρώτατον). On the various legends concerning the apostles and their supposed destinations see Elliott-Binns, *The Beginnings of Western Christendom*, p. 90.

likely that they returned to Galilee; for all of them, save Judas the man of Kerioth, were Galileans by birth and upbringing, though Andrew and Philip had Greek names (cf. John 12.20ff). Not every one of them, one may suppose, possessed the energy and initiative of St Peter. The prophecy of Matt. 10.23 that the apostles would not have completed the evangelization of the cities of Israel before the coming of the end seems to support this assumption.[1]

That the original community at Jerusalem grew up round a small group of Galileans who had there taken up their abode seems very likely,[2] with St Peter as their leader. The Church thus owed its initial impulse to the impression made by Jesus on His immediate followers. But after no long interval conditions arose which brought about a striking change in the position which the original leaders occupied in the Church, and they sank back into relative, if not absolute, unimportance. *Christianisme apostolique* was displaced by *Christianisme dynastique*, to adopt terms used by Goguel.[3]

Many reasons have been suggested to account for this transformation of the Church in Jerusalem. Probably behind it lay a change in the membership of the community. The Jews who joined the Church (even if the numbers of Acts 2.41; 4.4 are exaggerated they were, doubtless, a considerable body) must have had a very different outlook from that of the Galileans who were its earliest members. This would be true above all of the 'great number' of priests (Acts 6.7) who would bring with them a subtle, though far-reaching, difference. In Acts 8.1 it is stated that *all* the Church, except the apostles, were scattered owing to the persecution over Stephen.[4] This statement is certainly exaggerated, though their numbers must have been large since some of them went as far as Phœnicia, Cyprus, and Antioch (Acts 11.19). It is probable that the Hellenists alone were affected.

---

[1] W. L. Knox, *op. cit.*, p. 247, suggested that after leaving Jerusalem they may have had definite districts assigned to them, the forerunners of the later dioceses, for purposes of organization.

[2] Cf. Goguel, *L'Église Primitive*, p. 26.

[3] *La Naissance du Christianisme*, pp. 129ff. Goguel's theory is favourably regarded by Marcel Simon (*The Modern Churchman*, 1951, p. 50).

[4] W. Manson, *The Epistle to the Hebrews*, chapter ii, suggests that the speech of Stephen was a call to the Church to leave the narrow confines of Judaism and set forth on the mission to the Gentiles.

This must have seriously altered the balance of the Church, and the apostles may have fallen under criticism for having been responsible for the appointment of the Seven (Acts 6.3). Moreover as Galileans, and not interested in organization (Acts 6.2), the apostles must have found the growing tendency to rigidity a little oppressive. Except St Peter and St John they were probably not men of any force of character and possessed little learning. None of them would make any contribution to the literature of the N.T., and though the names of Peter and John are attached to certain books the attribution is far from being accepted by all scholars, and in the case of St John is rejected by the majority. In the eyes of those who had undergone a very different training they must have seemed ignorant and insignificant. Perhaps too the habitual contempt of the inhabitants of Jerusalem for all Galileans may not have been entirely abolished when they adopted Christianity. There may also have been a different attitude towards the temple cultus. Men whose whole lives had been spent under the shadow of the temple could not fail to regard it with reverence; the original disciples, and possibly Jesus Himself, may not have shared their views.[1] That the apostles took a predominant part in the pre-institutional period of the life of the Church in Jerusalem is beyond question, but as its leadership became more priestly and less prophetic they would gradually be pushed into the background. They were missionaries and evangelists, witnesses to what they had seen and known, but with no desire or perhaps capacity for administration.

The delay in the return of the Master may have had a double effect upon their position. On the one hand, since the expectation of a speedy return presumably depended on the teaching of the Twelve, its postponement would tend to diminish confidence in their guidance. On the other hand, it would make urgent a more elaborate organization such as had seemed needless when there was a belief in the close imminence of the parousia.

Harnack thought that the departure of the apostles from Jerusalem was due to 'strained relations unknown to us' (*The Constitution and Law of the Church*, p. 33), and Lietzmann saw in Rev.

---

[1] So Lohmeyer, *Kultus und Evagelium*, suggests. The Ebionites considered that Jesus sought to abolish the sacrificial system. Opposition to the temple cult was also found in some Jewish sects and Schoeps thinks that traces of it may be found in the Dead Sea Scrolls.

21.14 'the reflection of opposing tendencies in Jerusalem at an early date', for though the names of the apostles are written on the twelve foundation stones of the heavenly Jerusalem it is the four and twenty elders who sit on thrones near the Lamb (*The Beginnings of the Christian Church*, p. 84). In Acts 11.30 the elders occupy an important place in the Church.

It is a modern fashion to seek for economic causes to explain historical happenings; a procedure which has much to commend it, though when applied too drastically it is apt to provoke a reaction. That the displacement of the Twelve by St James may have been due, at least in part, to such causes is suggested by a certain amount of evidence. The outpouring of the Spirit on the day of Pentecost was followed by a great burst of 'enthusiasm' and by some unhealthy excitement; the continuance of such a state may have led the Church of Jerusalem, or many of its members, to disregard temporal concerns, which in any case were of no great account in view of the expectation that the return of the Lord would take place almost immediately. A system of voluntary communism seems to have been adopted, an extension, it may be, of the methods by which our Lord and His disciples had been supported by wealthy women in Galilee (Luke 8.1-3) and these were now present in Jerusalem (Luke 23.55; Acts 1.14). Those who benefited from it no doubt included the Galileans who had made Jerusalem their home. Although there seems to have been no compulsion on the part of the rich to help the rest,[1] many, carried away by the wave of generous feeling, would do so. But the sale of possessions involved a loss of capital, and when it was exhausted those who had depended on charity, some of whom may have ceased to work (cf. II Thess. 3.10ff), would have small chance of obtaining employment in Jerusalem. There seems, indeed, to have been an economic collapse which called for the alms of other Churches. The expulsion of the Seven, who had been responsible for financial administration,[2] must also have caused much dislocation. As they had been appointed by the

---

[1] Ananias had a free choice (Acts 5.4). Goguel, *L'Église Primitive*, p. 566, points out that Mary, the mother of Mark, evidently kept her property (Acts 12.2).

[2] B. S. Easton, *Early Christianity*, p. 78, thought that 'in the source from which Luke drew his information the Seven were not "deacons" at all: they were the leaders . . . of Greek-speaking Jerusalem Christians'. In this case they would have been preachers and missionaries, not administrators.

Twelve the latter may have been blamed for the economic difficulties.

The exact date of St James's succession to the leadership is not known; it may have followed on the death of Stephen and the expulsion of the Hellenists.[1] When St Paul went up to Jerusalem after his conversion it was to see Cephas, and though James is also mentioned he was evidently of less importance and dignity (Gal. 1.18f). On his visit fourteen (or perhaps eleven) years later James is given the first place (Gal. 2.9), although Cephas receives separate mention in vv.7f, presumably on account of his missionary activities.[2] It is possible that St Peter, like St Paul, was only present in Jerusalem on a temporary visit on this occasion, which may have been the holding of the council described in Acts 25.[3] The previous flight of St Peter, probably with that of the other apostles (Acts 12.1ff), would leave St James as the sole leader, though v.17 suggests that he already occupied that position.[4]

The rise of St James to prominence must have been comparatively late, otherwise his name would have been considered as a successor to Judas (Acts 1.14, 23ff). He certainly possessed the qualification of having seen the risen Lord (I Cor. 15.7). When James, the brother of John, was slain no attempt seems to have been made to fill up the number of the Twelve, or at least we have no record of such an attempt[5]; it is, however, possible that St James was chosen in the place of his namesake. The two are often confused in early Christian literature.[6]

The failure to fill up the number of the Twelve suggests a shifting of interest; the desire henceforth was not to continue the

[1] Cf. C. H. Turner in *J.T.S.*, I, pp. 55off.

[2] Oscar Cullmann, *Peter, Disciple-Apostle-Martyr*, considers that St Peter, after being head of the Church, later became the leader of the Jewish Christian expansion which was based on and directed by the Jerusalem Church. In Acts 8.14 Peter, with John, is *sent* by the apostles to Samaria.

[3] Kirsopp Lake considered that the 'famine-relief' visit (Acts 11.29f) and that to attend the council were one and the same (*Beginnings of Christianity*, V, pp. 468f); a conclusion held earlier by Spitta and others.

[4] B. S. Easton, *op. cit.*, pp. 73f, thought that James became president of the presbytery at Jerusalem and ruler of the Church (in conjunction with the elders) in imitation of the High Priest, who though not an elder presided over the Jerusalem Sanhedrin and was the head of the Jews as a whole. Hegesippus (in Eusebius *Hist. Eccles.* II.xxiii.4) stated that James held rule jointly with the apostles.

[5] See above, p. 54 note 1.

[6] As in the *Gospel according to the Hebrews*, where St James is said to have been present at the Last Supper.

apostolic succession, but to perpetuate the office of Christ Himself in His own family (an abortive anticipation of the caliphate of Islam) just as the Jewish priesthood had been perpetuated in the family of Aaron. Others, moved by vague nationalist hopes, may have attached value to the Davidic descent of the relations of Jesus.

St James was certainly well fitted to take over the guidance of the infant Church at this time of crisis; personal merit, as well as his relationship to Jesus, may have been a strong factor in the choice, and must have made his administration more acceptable. He was evidently a statesman and a steadying force, and seems to have been not averse to compromise even with Pauline Christianity, though his representatives may not have been equally tactful (Gal. 2.12). It was not without importance that he was *persona grata* with the Jewish authorities, especially with the Pharisees.[1] St James himself may well have been a Pharisee before his conversion, and his original hesitation in accepting the claims of Jesus was perhaps due to a fear of dangerous innovations, natural in one whose religious views were strictly orthodox and perhaps a little rigid.

According to St Paul (I Cor. 9.5) the brethren of the Lord became active missionaries. Lohmeyer, *Galiläa und Jerusalem*, p. 53, says that they took part in mission preaching from the first (*von Anfang an*); but that is an extension of St Paul's statement for which we have no evidence. How they came to believe we are not informed. As pious Jews they would be present at the Passover in Jerusalem, going up with their own friends and acquaintances (cf. Luke 2.44), and when Jesus was arrested and condemned they may well have been drawn to see the end of their brother. His death may thus have made a deep impression upon them, and still more the knowledge that He had risen again.[2] They had already joined the Church soon after the ascension (Acts 1.14) and were presumably present on the day of Pentecost. But, apart from St James, the N.T. tells us nothing more about them.

That one who had not believed in Jesus during His ministry should supplant the original disciples in the leadership of the

---

[1] His murder was the work of a fanatical section of the Jews and was lamented by the majority (see Josephus *Ant.* XX.ix.1).

[2] But 'my brethren' in Matt. 28.10 can only refer to the disciples, not the kinsmen, of Jesus.

Church is an astounding thing, and it is exceedingly likely that it caused intense resentment, if not among the Twelve, yet among their fellow Galileans. This may be the reason why there are in all the Gospels (including John 7.5)[1] derogatory references to the kindred of Jesus. Some critics think that they were mere inventions, but this can hardly have been the case. The fact, however, that they were remembered and recorded shews that feeling against them must have existed in certain quarters, otherwise their early unbelief and action against Jesus would have been quietly passed over. Such is, of course, far from being the case. But the sources behind the Synoptics, and possibly the Gospels of Mark and Matthew, go back before the fall of Jerusalem; thus it follows that accounts of the unbelief of the brethren of the Lord were openly disseminated at a time when they must have been leading members of the Church at Jerusalem and highly respected by the Church as a whole.

Though there is a casual mention of the unbelief of the brethren in the fourth Gospel much greater emphasis is laid upon it in the Synoptists. It seems to me that there is intentional significance to be found in the fact that the account of the choice of the Twelve in Mark 3.16-19 is almost immediately followed by the contrasted attitude of the relations of Jesus. Significant also is the value attached to spiritual, as distinguished from natural, relationship (e.g. Mark 3.21, 31ff, 6.4); any claims based on physical relationship are decisively rejected by Jesus. It must not, however, be forgotten that Mark makes no attempt to conceal the shortcomings and blindness of the disciples (e.g. Mark 4.40; 7.18; 8.17f, 21, 32f), though some passages which might seem to endanger the prestige of the Twelve are modified in Matthew and Luke.[2]

That a number of different parties existed in the primitive Church cannot be denied—though Eph. 4.4 could speak of 'one faith'—and we have already noted that even among Jewish Christians there were various outlooks. In the earliest days, before the admission of the Gentiles, one later point of dispute could not

---

[1] Goguel, *La Naissance du Christianisme*, pp. 282f, considers that after A.D. 70 the apostolic tradition was preserved at Ephesus. This might account for the inclusion in the fourth Gospel.

[2] Cf. Mark 4.10 and Matt. 4.52; Mark 4.13 and Matt. 13.16f. Mark 8.17 is omitted Matt. 16.9 (cf. 12). Luke omits Mark 4.13; 6.52; 8.17; 9.10; 10.24, 32, 35-45, and changes 4.40, and explains away 9.32.

have arisen—that over circumcision as a necessary preliminary to admission to the Church—for all would be circumcised. It was this question which attained major importance and even threatened to split the Church. There may have been other equally significant differences between those Christians who looked to St Paul, and the rest. Paul himself claimed that the gospel which he preached had not been received from man, but had come by direct revelation (Gal. 1.12ff). This can hardly mean anything less than that he introduced, as a consequence of the revelation which he had received, some new element into the gospel message. Was it a new way of approach, a gospel especially intended to appeal to the Gentiles?

By about the middle of the first century three distinct groups[1] had apparently emerged. (*a*) That in Jerusalem of which St James was the leader; a group which kept in close touch with the Jews and held as far as possible to the old ways, and advanced very slowly and cautiously; concerned perhaps above all else to preserve the rights of the Holy City as the headquarters of the new People of God. (*b*) The Pauline Churches with their liberal outlook and much larger proportion of Gentile members, and an ever-growing tendency to move away from Judaism and towards a freer interpretation of the Gospel. (*c*) The Christians in Galilee representing the first followers of Jesus, proud of their spiritual past and jealous of the position of Jerusalem. They may well have included some of the Twelve, possibly St Peter among them.[2]

These divisions are perhaps reflected in the Church of Corinth. The Christ party (I Cor. 1.12) may conceivably represent the Galilean standpoint and denote those who had been personal followers of Christ[3]; Baur, however, identified it with the Cephas

---

[1] The division into three groups is accepted by Harnack and by Streeter, but they differ from those suggested above. For Harnack they were (*a*) the Twelve; (*b*) the apostles (i.e. missionaries); (*c*) the rest of the disciples (*The Constitution and Law of the Church*, pp. 7f). These groups depend on function, not on difference of outlook. Streeter's three groups are (*a*) The Progressives, represented by St Paul; (*b*) the Conservatives, represented by St James; and (*c*) the Moderates, represented by St Peter (*The Four Gospels*, p. 545).

[2] Mark, which is supposed to represent the standpoint of St Peter, supports the Galilean tradition against that of Jerusalem.

[3] I am inclined to think that there was no 'Christ party'; and that the expression 'I am of Christ' was intended as a condemnation of those who had taken to them merely human leaders; cf. Otto Pfleiderer, *Paulinismus*, p. 316.

party; but others have seen in this party a suspicion on the part of some that St Peter had deviated from the original teaching of Jesus.[1] Then, in addition to the followers of St Paul, there was the obscure group which held to Apollos. Apollos we are told elsewhere had been baptized by John the Baptist and later instructed in the way of the Lord (Acts 18.25, κατηχημένος τὴν ὁδὸν τοῦ κυρίου). It may be that, although willing to accept Jesus as the Messiah, he considered his original baptism was sufficient; after all, Jesus Himself had submitted to it (Matt. 3.13-15). It is strange, however, that, if he had been instructed by a Christian catechist (if, indeed, that is the meaning of κατηχεῖν),[2] there had been no insistence on baptism in the name of Christ.

The division of the primitive Church into distinct groups or parties, though there might be fierce conflict between the Judaizers and the more liberal school, did not among the leaders at any rate involve any quarrel or severance of relations; they could agree to differ, and still co-operate (Gal. 2.9). Differences of policy might lead to temporary coolness, as in the case of St Paul and St Barnabas (Acts 15.36ff), but this was later overcome. St Paul's mention of Cephas and James (I Cor. 15.5, 7) as witnesses to the resurrection shews that he, at least, bore them no ill-will. If the writer of James was typical of the community which he addressed no desire to emphasize differences characterized it. Such differences as existed (cf. Jas. 4.1) seem to have been personal rather than doctrinal. The writer seems to have been content to hold firmly to his own views, but to have had no wish to engage in controversy. There may, however, be evidence in the epistle of reluctance to increase the prestige of Jerusalem, for its name is not found in Jas. 5.12 although it occurs in the parallel passage in Matt. 5.35. The mention in the latter, however, may be an addition.

We have thus evidence of differences between the Twelve and the Church at Jerusalem, with the subordination of the former, so far as organization at least is concerned; and following on

---

[1] As there is no evidence that St Peter was ever in Corinth, T. W. Manson, *Sayings of Jesus*, p. 203, suggests that the Cephas party 'seem to stand for claims on behalf of Peter to have some kind of oversight of Gentile churches'.

[2] It is so taken by A. Wright, 'Apollos: a study in Pre-Pauline Christianity' in *Expos. Times*, Oct. 1897. Ed. Meyer, *Ursprung und Anfänge*, I, p. 7, rejected the notion that it had any technical meaning.

that the probability of resentment on the part of the Galilean Christians. But strangely enough 'in ecclesiastical tradition it is Peter and Paul, the two great missionaries, not James, who are the chief of the Apostles'.[1] How did this come about? It seems to me that it was in part the consequence of the increasingly Gentile composition of the Church, in part the result of the impressions created by the Fall of Jerusalem in A.D. 70.

The Fall of Jerusalem itself is strangely ignored in the N.T., and Professor Brandon is quite right in drawing attention to its importance.[2] For our purposes it had two most important consequences: (*a*) It discredited the rigid party of Jewish Christians at Jerusalem who had highly valued the temple and its sacrifices[3]; (*b*) it seemed a judgement on the Law, and so a confirmation of the teaching of St Paul. A natural sequel was that St James should lose his prestige among Christians in general, especially among the growing Gentile majority, and become a figure of only secondary importance.[4] He might continue to be revered by many Jewish Christians, though scarcely by the Galileans who had been in opposition to him during his lifetime.

[1] Kirsopp Lake in *The Beginnings of Christianity*, V, p. 59.
[2] See *The Fall of Jerusalem and the Christian Church*. Although I recognize the value of Professor Brandon's work I am not at all convinced of the validity of all his arguments.
[3] The opinion of Montefiore of its effects on the Jews is worth quoting in this connexion. He considered that 'the crowning mercy of Judaism was the destruction of the Temple and the consequent obligatory cessation of animal sacrifices and of the functions of the Priesthood' (in *Record and Revelation*, p. 439).
[4] Traces of deliberate attempts to belittle St James are to be found in later writings: cf. *Syn. Script. Sacrae* appended to the writings of St Athanasius (Migne, *Pat. Gr.* IV, col. 432) where it is affirmed that he owed his position in Jerusalem to the appointment of the apostles.

VI

THE MIGRATION TO PELLA

AFTER the death of Herod Agrippa in A.D. 44 parts of Galilee seem to have been in a state of continual unsettlement and even of a species of guerilla warfare.[1] This continued up to the final revolt of 66. Like Macduff, men must have felt that 'confusion now hath made his masterpiece' (*Macbeth* II.iii.72). Normal life was seriously interrupted by robber bands who preyed on the inhabitants in the name of patriotism,[2] and the condition of many unfortunate lands in our own day will furnish a ready illustration of what life means in such circumstances. The more zealous nationalists, whilst holding apocalyptic notions of Israel's coming restoration, were not content to leave its realization solely to the divine intervention; they themselves would attempt to hasten it. Others adopted a 'scorched earth' policy and refused to sow their lands (Josephus *Ant.* XVIII.viii.3, *Bell. Jud.* II.x.5). Such ideas found a more eager reception in Galilee than in Jerusalem, until the latter came under the power of Galileans such as John of Giscala (*Bell. Jud.* IV.ii.1ff). For Jews who were unwilling to throw in their lot with the extremists Galilee must have been an exceedingly unpleasant place to live in, and those who cherished genuine and spiritual religion, both Jews and Christians, must have found it a dark age, an age when 'the spirit is narrowed and confined, and the stars are visible at noonday'.

The outbreak of the revolt against Rome was disgraced by a number of massacres of Gentiles, though in Caesarea it was the Jews who were the victims. The punitive expedition sent by the Romans met with little resistance until it arrived before Jerusa-

---

[1] The outlying districts with a sparse population would alone be affected at first. No such unsettlement is reflected in the gospels, though Dodd, *The Parables* etc., p. 125, suggests that it may be found in Mark 12 (the wicked husbandmen), nor in James (4.1 is figurative).
[2] The Jews themselves were the chief sufferers from acts which were ostensibly aimed at the occupying power; see *Ant.* XVII.x.8.

lem. It was then compelled to retreat, and great disorders followed in Galilee. Josephus went there to organize the resistance movement and claimed to have fortified many cities and to have raised an army of ten thousand men. Then early in 67 Vespasian invaded Palestine and quickly reduced the Galilean strongholds. Some cities of Galilee, however, including Sepphoris the former capital of the Herods, took the Roman side. The outcome of the struggle was immense suffering and damage for the Jewish people in Palestine. Most of those who escaped death were sold into slavery and there was much destruction of property. Albright, *Archaeology of Palestine*, p. 241, says that 'not a single synagogue of the early Roman period has been discovered in any part of Palestine . . . the native population ruthlessly massacred the Jews and destroyed their homes and public buildings. . . . [After the revolt] the principal focus of Jewish life shifted to the Coastal Plain around Joppa and Lydda.'

In the prevailing conditions the Christian Church must have been faced by innumerable difficulties and its further development and growth have been seriously hindered. There must also have been grave problems for individual Christians. More and more men's minds would be obsessed by nationalistic ambitions, and dreams of political liberty would displace the desire for spiritual freedom. It is probable that some Jewish Christians were swept away on the swiftly flowing tide of nationalism, but they can hardly have been very numerous. Eisler, however, held that the Jewish followers of Jesus proclaimed a doctrine of political, not spiritual, liberation and looked forward to His return to deliver Israel from its oppressors, just as the Welsh, in the Middle Ages, believed that King Arthur would return to free them from the English yoke. (*The Messiah Jesus*, pp. 539f.) Eisler's views have been accepted by Brandon, and with some reservations by Schonfield, *History of Jewish Christianity*, pp. 20f; but they have been subjected to damaging criticism by Schoeps in *The Journal of Eccles. Hist.*, iii, p. 102 and by Marcel Simon in *The Modern Churchman*, 1951, p. 51. They are based on the acceptance of the *Testimonia Flaviana* and the Slavonic version of Josephus's *Wars*, and involve a rejection of the testimony of Acts. Few scholars, however, look upon the Slavonic version as genuine, and even if it were, it would represent no more than the opinion of one who had no sympathy with the Christians and was only too ready to fall in with Roman views. There is also a further difficulty. If the Jewish Christians had been revolutionaries the Romans would have taken strong measures against them, and there is no scrap of evidence that they did so. Any persecution would have been sure to have left traces in the N.T. and other early Christian writings.[1]

Eusebius, after recalling various outrages against the Church— the deaths of Stephen, of James, the son of Zebedee, and of James, the first bishop of Jerusalem—goes on to relate that warned by an oracle the Christians of Jerusalem fled to a city of Peraea which they called Pella. After their flight, and after holy men had abandoned not only Jerusalem but the whole of Judaea, the divine justice took vengeance on the Jews for their acts of violence against Christ and His apostles (*Hist. Eccles.* III.v.2f). This account is almost certainly derived from Hegesippus, from whose memoirs Eusebius seems to have borrowed the narrative of the martyrdom of James. The same source seems also to underlie the three descriptions of the flight to Pella in Epiphanius (*Haer.* XXIX.7, XXX.2, *De Mens. et Pond.* XV.2-5).[2]

The flight to Pella is rejected by Brandon, *The Fall of Jerusalem* etc., pp. 168ff, following Eisler, but his views have not found much favour with other scholars.[3] One of his arguments is that the Christians of Jerusalem would not have chosen so Gentile a centre (p. 169). But as Pella was sacked by the Jews in 66 (*Bell. Jud.* II.xviii.1) few Gentiles may have remained there. He also exaggerates the good feeling of the Jews in Jerusalem towards the Church. That conservative Jews may have venerated St James is most likely; but they themselves were losing control of affairs, and some Jews, Johanan ben Zakkai for example, themselves fled from Jerusalem; so in earlier days the Zadokite sect had sought refuge in distant Damascus, and they were most pious Jews. Persecution by the zealots could best be avoided by migration to some place outside Jewish control, and safety would be more certain within the Roman sphere of influence. That there were communities of Jewish Christians in Pella and its neighbourhood in later times is beyond all question; it is a reasonable

---

[1] Such persecutions as are there recorded were at the hands of the Jews.
[2] See further Lawlor, *Eusebiana*, pp. 27-34.
[3] They are rejected by Schoeps and by Marcel Simon. So far as I know Eisler was the first to throw doubt on the flight.

assumption that they included descendants of the fugitives from the troubles of 67.

The district of Peraea, although it is linked to Galilee geographically by only a narrow strip, must have been very familiar to Galileans, for many pilgrims to Jerusalem preferred to cross over the Jordan and travel through Peraea so as to avoid the journey through Samaria. Its Jewish character is recognized in the Mishnah where it is frequently grouped with Judaea and Galilee as forming one of the three divisions of Jewish Palestine. Pella itself, like the neighbouring Dion, was probably founded by veterans of the armies of Alexander the Great and named from his birthplace in Macedonia. It had once been a thriving town with noble buildings, but was destroyed by Alexander Jannaeus because the inhabitants refused to accept the Law (*Ant*. XIII. xv.3f, *Bell. Jud*. I.iv.8). Pella, which Pliny included among the cities of the Decapolis (*Hist. Nat*. v.18, 74), was linked with the outer world by the highway from Scythopolis to Damascus. It occupied a healthy site with a good water supply and was surrounded by fertile country. Its great disadvantage, in the absence of a strong protecting power, was liability to raids from the desert.

That Christianity had reached the neighbourhood before the flight in 67 is highly probable; the Arabians mentioned in Acts 2.11 may well have come from near-by districts. If this were the case the choice of Pella seems natural. Renan, long ago, found a reference to the Jewish Christians in Pella in Rev. 12.1ff, 13ff, and his suggestion is regarded with favour by R. H. Charles; they were safe in the desert whilst other Christians had to endure hardships.

Eusebius's account of the flight implies that it was not from Jerusalem alone that the refugees were drawn to Pella; other parts of Judaea also supplied their quota. Doubtless they included men and women from Galilee, for the land across the Jordan was traditionally a haven for those who wished to escape from troubles in Palestine (cf. II Sam. 2.8; 4.22-24). The district was overrun by Vespasian in the spring of 68 (*Bell. Jud*. IV.vii.3ff), but it is unlikely that Jewish Christians, who would offer no resistance to the Romans, suffered much damage or hurt.

If the refugees at Pella included, as seems almost certain, members both of the Church at Jerusalem and Christians from Galilee, it is not unreasonable to suppose that the two communities would be drawn closely together and differences between them be forgotten in their common misfortunes.

There is a passage in Eusebius (III.xi) which may contain evidence of such a drawing together; but it is so obscure and unreliable that little value can be attached to it. Like other similar matter it seems to be derived from Hegesippus. He tells us that following the murder of James and the capture of Jerusalem, which he places immediately after that event (τὴν αὐτίκα γενομένην), the surviving apostles and disciples of Jesus assembled from all parts and with His kinsmen after the flesh, most of whom were still living, elected Symeon, the son of Clopas, as the successor of James in the bishopric of Jerusalem.

Before going on to discuss the exact meaning of the three classes into which the electors were divided, certain difficulties may be pointed out. The first is the time of the election which Eusebius places subsequent to the fall of Jerusalem. His whole chronology, however, in this passage is open to criticism for, as we have seen, he places the death of James and the fall of Jerusalem in close juxtaposition. In reality there was a gap of at least eight years between them, for James was martyred in 61 or 62, and the city was not finally captured until 70.[1] Hort, who rejected as incredible the dating of the election after the fall, suggested that Eusebius may have taken a rhetorical use of καὶ εὐθύς by Hegesippus too literally (*Judaistic Christianity*, p. 171). The actual date was probably at no long interval after the death of James and therefore before the siege had begun. Where the election took place we are not told, but in the eyes of Eusebius it cannot have been Jerusalem which would then have been in the possession of the Romans and in a state of disturbance.

Thus Eusebius (and Hegesippus behind him) does not provide certain evidence of united action by the various groups in the election of Symeon. At the same time the account need not be entirely dismissed. It testifies to a tradition that these various groups had been drawn together in this period. To discuss them will not be wasted labour.

---

[1] In IV.xxii.4 where Hegesippus is directly quoted there is no mention of the Fall, nor of a gathering of electors; see Lawlor, *Eusebiana*, pp. 18ff.

The three groups were: (*a*) The apostles; (*b*) the personal followers of Jesus; (*c*) the kinsmen of Jesus. (*a*) What is signified by 'the apostles'? Presumably Eusebius refers to those mentioned in III.v.2 as having been driven out of Judaea into all parts of the world. But if the reference is to the Twelve it is strange that they should be distinguished from the next group, the personal followers of Jesus. May it not be that the term has here no technical sense,[1] but represents rather what we should now call missionaries, those who had been sent forth into foreign parts by the home Church to preach the Gospel, and who were then recalled to take their share in the important business of electing a new head for the mother Church at Jerusalem? (*b*) The mention of the personal followers of Jesus implies that there was a definite body who stood apart from the rest of the Christian community and were so distinguished. Is it not possible, not to say probable, that they represented the Christians of Galilee who, above all others, would deserve such a title? (*c*) The kinsmen of Jesus are a clearly defined body; they formed a separate group in Acts 1.14 and also I Cor. 9.5 where mention is made of their missionary activity. Eusebius (I.vii.14), quoting a letter of Africanus to Aristides, says that some of them came from Nazareth and Kocheba. They seem to have been suspected of trading on their relationship (11). Under Domitian they were apparently simple souls more interested in agriculture than in the propagation of Christianity, and hardly the type from which religious leaders would be expected to emerge (Eusebius III.xixf.). Yet Hegesippus records that they 'ruled every church as being witnesses (or martyrs) and of the family of the Lord' (III.xxxii.6).

[1] A similar, non-technical use in other passages is suggested by Harnack, *The Constitution* etc., p. 7 and by Rawlinson, *St Mark* (Westminster Commentaries), p. 83.

VII

THE LATER HISTORY
OF THE GALILEAN CHRISTIANS

ALTHOUGH it lies somewhat outside our enquiry a brief survey of the subsequent history of Jewish Christianity, especially in Galilee itself, is of interest and may throw light on the earlier period with which we are concerned.

After the fall of Jerusalem and the restoration of Roman government a number of Christians returned to the city from Pella[1]; some of them, 'disciples of the disciples', were seen there by Aquilla the translator, if we can accept the rather dubious statement in the Syriac version of Epiphanius *De Mens. et Pond.* xv.[2] There seems, however, to have been no considerable return of Jews who were not Christians, for no Jewish tomb or inscribed ossuary dated after A.D. 70 has been found by archæologists.[3] Lightfoot thought that most of the Christian Jews returned to Jerusalem; speaking of the fourth-century sect of the Nazarenes in Peraea he wrote (*Galatians*, p. 318): 'Can we doubt that they were the remnant of the fugitive Church, which refused to return from their exile with the majority to the now Gentile city, some because they were too indolent or too satisfied to move, others because the abandonment of the law seemed too heavy a price to pay for Roman forbearance?'

Pella remained a Christian centre and gave at least one author to the early Church, Ariston, who wrote an apology in the form of a dialogue between a Hebrew Christian named Jason and a Jew of Alexandria named Papiscus. It is from this work most probably that Eusebius derived his reference to the rising of Bar Cochba (IV.vi.3).[4] Ariston's views were strictly orthodox and St Jerome (*Quaest. Hebr. in Gen.* III) drew attention to his explanation of

[1] See Hoennicke, *Judenchristentum*, pp. 105ff, and cf. Eusebius III.xi., IV.v.2.
[2] See P. de Lagarde, *Philologus*, XVIII, p. 352.
[3] Albright, *Arch. of Palestine*, p. 241.
[4] So Lawlor and Oulton, *Eusebius* II, pp. 122f.

Gen. 1.1 as meaning *In filio fecit Deus coelum et terram*. Renan *Les Évangiles*, p. 97, made the ingenious suggestion that it was in this region that the Gospel records were first reduced to writing by the refugees from Jerusalem, and in the Aramaic dialect which, he thought, differed but slightly from that of the inhabitants so far as they did not speak Greek. The Christians at Pella, however, contributed little to the general development of the Church as a whole, and since there were in its neighbourhood a number of Jewish sects, who had separated themselves in earlier times, its orthodoxy may have been corrupted by the infiltration of Essene and even Gnostic elements.[1]

What, it may next be asked, became of the fugitives from Galilee? Did they also return to their homes, or did they either remain in Pella or migrate with their fellow-exiles to Jerusalem? To such questions confident answers are, of course, impossible, for our knowledge is too scanty. The end of hostilities must have been followed by great hardships, houses and towns had been destroyed and the economic basis of life become precarious. But Galilee, having been occupied by the Romans quite early, was already on the way to recovery and conditions there were doubtless more stable than in Judaea. So it is probable that many Galilean Christians would return. At any rate it is certain that Christianity did not die out in Galilee. Capernaum,[2] for example, was regarded by the rabbis as a pestilential home of the *minim* (heretics, and especially Jewish Christians),[3] whilst the Talmud defined sinners as the sons of Kefar Nahum.[4]

There are a few notices of Galilee in Eusebius; he tells us, for instance, that relatives of Jesus were living there at the end of the first century (I.vii.13f), and in the previous chapter some further details about them are given. Melito of Sardis visited the Holy Land in the latter part of the second century in search of

---

[1] Cf., however, below p. 78.

[2] The exact site of Capernaum is not a matter of great importance for our purposes since all those proposed lie within a limited area. Masterman, *Studies in Galilee*, pp. 17ff, collected strong evidence in favour of Tell Hum, though he thought that the spelling should be Telhum (perhaps a corruption of Tankhum) as there is no trace of any tell in the locality. This identification is now generally accepted. G. A. Smith (*Hist. Geog. of the Holy Land*, p. 456 note) argues strongly for Khan Minyeh.

[3] The tradition seems to have persisted for G. A. Smith mentions that when Isaac Chilo visited the Holy Land in 1334 he knew of it.

[4] In Luke 7.11 two Old Latin MSS. substitute Capernaum for Nain. Is this evidence of a revived interest in the city?

books, but whether he enquired of Jews or Christians is uncertain (IV.xxvi.14). His contemporary Hegesippus was a Jew by origin (IV.xxii.8) and born in Palestine, perhaps in Galilee, and has handed down many traditions concerning the Church in Jerusalem; but no great confidence can be attached to his statements. Origen settled at Caesarea in 231 or 232 whence he exerted an immense influence. It was at Caesarea too that St Jerome discovered a copy of the *Gospel according to the Hebrews* (*De vir. illus.* iii, *Adv. Pelag.* iii.12); but how long it had been treasured there we do not know. Though Caesarea was not actually in Galilee influences emanating from it must have spread widely.

Some further information concerning Christianity in Galilee comes to us from rabbinic sources. In the early part of the second century there is mention of the somewhat elusive figure of Jacob of Kefar Sekanya (or Samma)[1] who performed works of healing in the name of Jesus (*Tos. Hullin* 22, *Qoh.* R. i.24). He was on friendly terms with the famous rabbi Eliezer ben Hyrcanus, a circumstance which led to the denunciation of the latter to the Roman authorities as a Christian.[2] But such intercourse between Christians and Jews must have been very rare, and Justin Martyr, himself a native of Samaria, tells us that Jews were forbidden to carry on disputes with Christians (*Dial.* xxxviii).

That Christianity should have found it difficult to recover lost ground in Galilee is not altogether surprising. Some Jewish Christians had doubtless been strongly attracted by nationalism and had perished in the struggle with Rome, some had remained beyond Jordan, but perhaps most significant of all was the fact that after the fall of Jerusalem Galilee became the centre of Jewish learning and religion. Judaea had been devastated and the atmosphere there was no longer favourable to quiet and study and so a new home for rabbinism had to be found. This was no easy task and *Rosh ha-Shanah* 31ab records ten migrations. From 70 to 135 Jamnia, near Jericho, was the principal headquarters; then there were moves to new centres in Galilee; at Usha, Sepphoris, and most famous of all, Tiberias. A school at Lydda in Judaea, however, was still kept up. Tiberias had been

---

[1] Perhaps Kefar Simai between Sepphoris and Acco.
[2] See Strack, *Einleitung in den Talmud*, p. 87, and W. A. L. Elmslie, '*Aboda Zara* (Texts and Studies, VIII, pt. 2), pp. 97f.

the home of Justus, Josephus' contemporary and rival, whose *History of the Jewish Kings* and *Jewish War* are now lost. Later it became the home of Rabbi Judah, the editor of the Mishnah, and for long retained a place apart in Jewish tradition. It was even said that there the Messiah would appear.[1]

The migration to Galilee must have been a sore trial to the rabbis who had hitherto regarded it as rude and unlearned[2]; now they were compelled to seek a refuge among its not very amenable inhabitants. Many of the rabbis, indeed, were shocked by the unwillingness of the people to receive their teaching, and Johanan ben Zakkai is reported to have exclaimed: 'O Galilee, Galilee, thou hatest the Law; thine end will be to have to deal with brigands.' (*Jer. Tal. Shabbath* 15d). But Jewish learning would take a still wider flight, for after 350 the Palestinian schools were closed and it then concentrated in Babylon.

When Willibald visited Palestine in 722 though he found many churches at Tiberias, there was only a single synagogue. Benjamin of Tudela in 1163 says that there were fifty Jews there, three of whom he named, and also the tomb of Johanan ben Zakkai.

The acceptance of Christianity by the Roman Empire must have led to an increase in the number of Christians in Galilee, but hardly among the Jewish population. The sudden popularity of the Holy Land as a place of pilgrimage led many to settle there, even from the West, though the neighbourhood of Jerusalem was naturally the favoured area, as with St Jerome. After the disputes of the West it seemed a blessed land of peace and holiness.

Then to his early home did love repair
And cheered his sickening heart with his own native air.

Epiphanius in the fourth century found little evidence of Christianity in Galilee. Gentiles, Samaritans, and Christians had been forbidden to settle in Tiberias, Nazareth, or Capernaum (*Haer.* XXX.xi), and he states that the first church to be built

---

[1] Stanley, *Sinai and Palestine*, p. 278.
[2] The lack of learning in Galilee may have been exaggerated, for Büchler, *Der galiläische 'Am-ha-'Ares*, pp. 274ff, claims that there were schools there before 136 and that many rabbis were Galileans both by birth and training. But the fact that the famous Jose the Galilean (early second century) was so named suggests that a Galilean rabbi was a *rara avis*.

was erected by a Jewish Christian named Joseph[1] in the time of Constantine (xii). On the other hand he has left it on record that Hebrew versions of John and Acts were preserved at Tiberias (iii).

Such revival of the Church in Galilee as took place was not to be of very long duration, for the Arab invasions of the seventh century struck it a cruel blow. Later would come the Crusades and the Latin kingdom of Jerusalem, providing a fresh Christian population. But they in turn were destined to be swept away for the most part, and in the end Christianity, like Buddhism, would almost disappear in the land of its origin.

Galilean Christianity was a form of Jewish Christianity in its origin, and so it remained. Something must therefore be said of the relations between Jewish Christians and Jews in general.

The appeal of Jesus had been to individuals, and the acceptance of His claim to be the Messiah did not necessarily involve dissociation with the national religious organization, perhaps not even for such priests as believed (Acts 6.7), and though there might be violence against Christians it seems to have been directed against Hellenists and those critical of the Mosaic Law.[2] Even the acceptance of Jesus as the Messiah was at first no insuperable barrier between Jews and Jewish Christians, for many had claimed to be the Messiah. Trouble over this matter seems to have come to a head in the days of Bar Cochba, whose claims were a challenge to all Jews and could not conceivably be accepted by the followers of Jesus. Because the Christians refused to fall into line they were tortured by his orders.[3] At a later time it would be affirmed, somewhat surprisingly, that the only real point of difference between Jews and Christians was the question of the Messiah (Tertullian *Apol.* xxi, *Adv. Jud.* vi, Hippolytus *Refut.* xiii-xxv, *Clem. Recog.* i.50).

The breach between the Church and the Jews came about

[1] Joseph is a very interesting figure. At first a rabbinic student at Tiberias he became a Christian and devoted himself to the building of churches where there were large Jewish populations, such as Tiberias, Nazareth and Sepphoris. For his services he was made a *comes* by Constantine.

[2] So Lietzmann, *The Beginnings of the Christian Church*, p. 90.

[3] Justin, *Apol.* I.xxxi. There is a possible reference to this in the second century *Apocalypse of Peter* where it is 'foretold' that when Christians rejected the false Messiah he would slay them with the sword and that martyrs would be many (James *Apoc. N.T.* pp. 511f). Some scholars see in John 5.43 a reference to the claims of Bar Cochba and possible Christian acceptance of his claims; but such a reference is highly improbable on chronological grounds.

gradually. But both sides had their share in it. Marcel Simon points out the difference of attitude between the treatment of the Jewish question in Hebrews and in the *Epistle of Barnabas*. In the former document the whole matter is an internal one, but in the latter it has become a question between the Church and the Jews (*Verus Israel*, p. 91, note 6).

On the part of the Jews there was a similar development. The collapse of the revolt and the capture of Jerusalem in 70 had utterly discredited the apocalyptic party, henceforward Judaism would consolidate around Pharisaism and the position of Jewish Christians would become more difficult. The steps taken against the *minim* may not have been aimed at them exclusively,[1] but they would make it impossible for Jewish Christians to continue their attendance at the synagogues. There seems also to be a reference to them in II *Baruch* xli.3 (cf. lxxxiii.8) for the writer speaks of many who have forsaken the covenant and cast away the yoke of the Law. Although the attitude of the Jews to Gentile Christians lies outside our enquiry it is not unrelated to it, for the bitter hatred towards those (mainly Gentiles) who followed St Paul in a supposed belittling of the Law would be extended to their fellow countrymen who were content to be classed with them under the general name of Christians. There was also rivalry between Jews and Christians in the matter of converts. Duchesne *Hist. Ancienne de l'Église*, I, p. 568, held that the Jews by this time had abandoned attempts to proselytize, but Simon (*op. cit.*, pp. 315ff) brings evidence to shew that even after the crises of 70 and of 135 they were still active.

The fall of Jerusalem and its consequences rendered the position of Jewish Christians one of extraordinary difficulty and delicacy, and even attempts to estimate their numbers are hazardous (Ropes thought there were few only outside Palestine).[2] On the one hand the Church as a whole was passing under the control of Gentiles and being influenced by Hellenistic conceptions. On the other hand Judaism was becoming more strict and rigid, so that opportunities for gaining fresh converts from it practically ceased, though there was an occasional adherent; Symmachus at the end

---

[1] For a discussion of the various views on this matter see Simon, *op. cit.*, pp. 215ff.
[2] See 'The Singular Problem of the Epistle to the Galatians' in *Harvard Theo. Rev.* XIV.

of the second century, for example, was a Jewish Christian,[1] and Simon, *op. cit.*, p. 311, takes this as evidence of propaganda. But they could hardly hope even to keep up their numbers, and ultimately those who had represented primitive Christianity were reduced to a mere sect. 'The original church disappeared with the migration to Pella and the destruction of Jerusalem [thence forward] Jewish Christianity lacked not only a racial, but also a religious basis for its former claims and thus was forgotten by the church catholic' (Lietzmann, *op. cit.*, p. 243).

Such a fate seemed inevitable, for 'the rejection of the Judeo-Christian compromise was essential to the development of Christianity'.[2] Their condition, however, was pitiable, and unless we realize what the Law and the ancient Jewish tradition signified to the pious Jew we shall fail to understand what it meant for a Christian of Jewish birth and upbringing to be excluded from it. The Law might be a burden to St Paul and others, but for the great majority of Jews it was the joy and strength of life. To them Jesus had not come to destroy the Law but to fulfil it (Matt. 5.17). 'There is no more tragic group in Christian history than these unhappy people. They, who might have been the bridge between the Jewish and Gentile world were rejected by the Church in spite of their genuine belief in Jesus as the Messiah, and then by the Jews in spite of their loyalty to the Law.' (Parkes, *op. cit.*, p. 92.)

The question as to how far the Ebionites and the Jewish Christians represent the same body of people is difficult and complex and cannot here be discussed in detail.[3] Harnack, *Dogmengeschichte* (1909), I, p. 330 suggested that after 70 the term Jewish Christian should be reserved for the Ebionites,[4] though this type of Christianity went back much further. Both terms are rather

[1] Eusebius VI.xvii 'an Ebionite'; Epiphanius *De Mens. et Pond.* xvi says that he was originally a Samaritan.
[2] Parkes, *The Conflict of the Church and the Synagogue*, p. 29.
[3] Cf. *Encyclopædia of Religion and Ethics*, V, p. 139: 'Some Ebionites were hardly distinguishable from the first Jewish Christians, from men like St Peter and St James who endeavoured to combine the faith of Christ with the obligations of the Law and their national hopes.' A full discussion will be found in Schoeps, *Theologie und Geschichte des Judenchristentums*, and Simon, *Verus Israel*.
[4] Simon seems to take Ebionite in this sense: 'Judeo-Christianity represents only a very sporadic phenomenon, with little depth. Even in Palestine the Ebionites are, compared with the Great Church, a minority . . . condemned . . . to disappear sooner or later' (*op. cit.*, p. 313).

indefinite in their application. Jewish Christian might signify any Christian who was a Jew by birth, or it might be restricted to those who continued in full observance of Jewish ceremonies and regulations. In view of the wide diversity of views held by Jewish Christians (see above, p. 50) it would be a mistake to regard them as forming a single homogeneous sect. So, too, in regard to the Ebionites,[1] such evidence as we possess comes from writers who regarded them as heretics in whole or in part.[2] To the former group belong Irenaeus, Hippolytus, Pseudo-Tertullian, and Epiphanius; those who took a less unfavourable view are Justin Martyr, Origen,[3] Eusebius and St Jerome.

That the Ebionites were in direct succession to the early Jewish Christians in Palestine and its neighbourhood, as they asserted, is most probable. Lightfoot (*Galatians* p. 318 quoted above, p. 71) had no doubt that the fourth-century sect of the Nazarenes was descended from the fugitives to Pella, though Hort could find no evidence to support the idea (*Judaistic Christianity* p. 176). Communities such as the Ebionites develop in various ways according to the influences to which they are subjected and may easily stray into heresy if cut off from the central body of the Church. Schoeps, however, denies that the Ebionites were Gnostics, as has often been alleged; he considers that they were anti-Marcionite (*op. cit.*, pp. 305ff). He also distinguishes them from the Elkasites (*op. cit.*, pp. 325ff).

If the primitive believers in Galilee thus became Ebionites, and the evidence seems to favour the view, we are led on to an extraordinary paradox, for there can be but little doubt that the form of Christianity with which Mohammed was acquainted resembled that of some sects of Ebionites. Thus the development of Jewish Christianity reached its culmination in the precincts of Islam.[4]

[1] As to the origin and meaning of the term see Schoeps, *op. cit.*, pp. 279ff.

[2] The following are the passages which deal with them: Justin Martyr *Apol.* I, 47-9; Irenaeus I.xxvi.2, III.xi.7, xxi.1, IV.xxxiii.4, V.i.3; Origen *Contra Celsum* II.1, V.61, 65, *De Princip.* IV.22, *Hom. on Gen.* iii.5, *Jer.* xvii.12, *Mt.* xvi.12, xvii.12; Eusebius III.xxvii; Epiphanius XVIII.1, XXIX.7, XXX.2ff, XL.1; Jerome *Epist. ad Aug.* CXII.13.

[3] Origen distinguished between those who accepted the virgin birth and those who rejected it (*Contra Celsum*, V.65).

[4] See Schoeps, *op. cit.*, pp. 334ff, and Schlatter, *Die Entwicklung des jüd. Christentums zum Islam.*

INDEX OF BIBLICAL REFERENCES

79